Social Media

Everything You Need to Know to Get Started

Kiet Huynh

Table of Contents

Introduction

1.1 What Is X (Twitter) and Why It Matters

In today's fast-paced, digitally connected world, social media platforms have transformed how we communicate, interact, and consume information. Among these platforms, X— previously known as Twitter—stands out as a powerful tool for real-time updates, concise communication, and global networking. But what exactly is X, and why should you care about it?

X is a social media platform that enables users to post short messages, known as "tweets," to share thoughts, ideas, and updates with their followers. Initially limited to 140 characters, tweets have evolved to allow longer posts, but the platform's essence remains rooted in brevity and immediacy. Unlike other platforms that emphasize curated content or visuals, X focuses on real-time conversations, making it a unique space for news, trends, and public discourse.

The Core Purpose of X

At its core, X is about fostering connections and enabling dialogue. It provides a platform for individuals, businesses, influencers, and organizations to share their voices, engage with communities, and stay informed about topics of interest. Whether it's breaking news, live event updates, or trending memes, X serves as a pulse of what's happening in the world.

One of the platform's most defining characteristics is its openness. Unlike private messaging apps or closed groups, X operates in a largely public sphere, where anyone can interact with anyone else. This openness has made it a vital space for advocacy, social movements, and even global diplomacy. Hashtags such as #BlackLivesMatter or #MeToo started as movements on X before gaining worldwide recognition and sparking real-world action.

Why X Matters to You

1. **A Hub for Real-Time Information**: X is often the first place where breaking news surfaces. Journalists, reporters, and eyewitnesses frequently turn to the platform to share updates as events unfold. From sports scores to political announcements, X allows users to stay informed almost instantly.

For businesses, this means having a direct channel to monitor industry news, competitor updates, and customer feedback in real-time. For individuals, it's a way to stay connected with interests and communities that matter to them.

2. **A Platform for Expression and Visibility**: X democratizes visibility. Unlike traditional media channels that often require significant resources to reach an audience, anyone on X can gain traction and build a following. Viral tweets and trending hashtags have proven that even individuals without a large initial audience can influence public opinion and spark meaningful conversations.

This accessibility makes X an excellent platform for creative individuals, thought leaders, and professionals looking to establish their personal brand. By sharing insights, engaging with others, and leveraging the right strategies, users can amplify their voices and grow their reach.

3. **A Networking Tool**: In an increasingly interconnected world, networking is no longer confined to conferences or formal gatherings. X provides an informal yet effective way to connect with industry leaders, potential collaborators, and like-minded individuals.

By participating in Twitter Chats, engaging in conversations, or simply following and interacting with thought leaders, users can create meaningful connections that might otherwise be difficult to establish. For job seekers, X has also become a place to find opportunities, showcase expertise, and engage with potential employers.

4. **An Advertising and Marketing Powerhouse**: For businesses, X is more than just a social media platform; it's a powerful marketing tool. Brands use it to promote products, run campaigns, and engage directly with customers. The platform's real-time nature allows businesses to respond quickly to trends and interact with their audience authentically.

X Ads, combined with the ability to target specific demographics, have made it a go-to choice for businesses looking to drive engagement and conversions. From small startups to global corporations, X has proven to be an essential part of a successful marketing strategy.

The Evolution of X

Launched in 2006 as a microblogging platform, Twitter was initially dismissed by some as a niche tool for tech-savvy users. However, its unique format and real-time capabilities quickly gained traction. Over the years, the platform has undergone significant transformations, adding features such as expanded character limits, multimedia uploads, and advanced analytics tools.

The acquisition of Twitter by Elon Musk in 2022 marked another major turning point. Under Musk's leadership, the platform was rebranded as "X" and underwent various changes aimed at enhancing user experience and fostering innovation. The rebranding reflected Musk's vision of transforming X into more than a social media platform—a digital space for diverse activities, including payments, commerce, and more.

X's Global Impact

The global reach of X cannot be understated. With millions of daily active users across countries and cultures, the platform plays a crucial role in shaping narratives and driving discussions. It has been used to:

- Mobilize communities during crises (e.g., disaster relief efforts).

- Provide a voice for the underrepresented.

- Facilitate global movements for change.

For instance, during natural disasters like hurricanes or earthquakes, X has been a critical tool for real-time updates, rescue coordination, and resource sharing. Similarly, in political contexts, it has provided a space for dissenting voices to reach a global audience.

The Challenges of X

While X offers immense opportunities, it's not without challenges. The platform has faced criticism for issues like misinformation, cyberbullying, and algorithmic biases. As a user, it's essential to navigate X responsibly, critically evaluate information, and engage constructively.

X has introduced various tools to address these challenges, such as fact-checking labels, content moderation policies, and enhanced privacy settings. Understanding these features will empower you to use the platform more effectively while staying safe.

Conclusion

X (Twitter) is more than just a platform for tweets—it's a space where ideas converge, communities grow, and voices are amplified. Whether you're an individual looking to share your thoughts, a professional seeking to expand your network, or a business aiming to reach a broader audience, X offers tools and opportunities to help you succeed.

In the chapters that follow, we'll guide you through the process of mastering X, from setting up your account to growing your presence and engaging meaningfully with others. By the end of this book, you'll not only understand what makes X unique but also how to leverage it for personal and professional success.

1.2 Who This Book Is For

Social media has become a ubiquitous part of modern life, and X (formerly Twitter) stands out as one of the most influential platforms for communication, networking, and branding. This book, *Social Media X (Twitter): Everything You Need to Know to Get Started,* is crafted for a diverse audience with varying goals, experiences, and expectations. Whether you're a complete beginner looking to join the conversation, a small business owner seeking to expand your brand's reach, or a professional aiming to build a personal brand, this book is tailored to help you succeed.

For Social Media Newcomers

If you've never used X before, the platform might seem overwhelming at first glance. Terms like "tweet," "retweet," and "threads" might sound foreign, and the fast-paced nature of the platform can be intimidating. This book is your roadmap to understanding the basics. You'll learn how to create an account, navigate the interface, and start posting your thoughts confidently.

We understand that diving into a new social media platform can feel like stepping into uncharted waters. That's why this guide is structured to introduce you gradually, starting with the fundamental features before progressing to advanced strategies. By the time you finish, you'll have the skills to participate actively and meaningfully on X.

For Entrepreneurs and Small Business Owners

X is a powerful tool for businesses of all sizes, especially small businesses looking to make a big impact with limited resources. This book is designed for entrepreneurs who want to establish their brand, reach a wider audience, and connect with customers in real time.

You'll learn how to craft tweets that resonate with your target audience, leverage hashtags for visibility, and use analytics to measure your success. We'll also cover advertising options on X, giving you a cost-effective way to promote your products or services. Whether you're running a local bakery, offering consulting services, or launching an online store, this book will equip you with the tools to use X effectively as part of your marketing strategy.

For Professionals Building a Personal Brand

In today's digital age, having a personal brand is more important than ever. X provides a unique opportunity to showcase your expertise, network with industry leaders, and establish yourself as a thought leader in your field.

This guide is ideal for professionals who want to use X to enhance their careers. From crafting compelling posts to engaging with relevant communities, we'll show you how to position yourself as an authority in your industry. You'll also learn how to use tools like threads to share in-depth insights and Spaces to host live discussions, enabling you to connect with your audience on a deeper level.

For Students and Job Seekers

Are you a student or job seeker looking to stand out in a competitive job market? X can be a valuable resource for networking, learning, and building your professional reputation. Many companies and recruiters actively use the platform to find talent and share job opportunities.

In this book, you'll discover how to use X to connect with professionals in your field, participate in relevant discussions, and showcase your skills. We'll also guide you on using the platform responsibly, ensuring that your online presence reflects your aspirations and professionalism.

For Creators and Influencers

If you're a content creator, writer, artist, or aspiring influencer, X offers a platform to share your work and grow your following. The platform's short-form content format encourages creativity and rapid engagement, making it an excellent space to showcase your talent.

This book will teach you how to create captivating content that drives engagement, use visuals effectively, and build a loyal audience. We'll also explore monetization opportunities, such as the Creator Program and sponsored posts, helping you turn your passion into a sustainable career.

For Businesses and Marketing Teams

Marketing professionals and teams will find this book an essential guide to understanding and leveraging X as part of a broader digital marketing strategy. From creating a content calendar to analyzing campaign performance, we'll cover everything you need to know to run successful marketing campaigns on the platform.

You'll learn how to integrate X with other marketing channels, engage with your audience authentically, and stay on top of trends to keep your brand relevant. Whether you're managing a corporate account or promoting a small business, this book provides actionable insights to maximize your results.

For Casual Users Looking to Stay Informed

Not everyone uses X for professional reasons, and that's okay. If you're simply looking for a way to stay informed, connect with friends, or share your thoughts, this book has you covered.

You'll learn how to customize your feed to see the content you care about most, participate in trending conversations, and discover communities that share your interests. X is a fantastic platform for finding real-time news, engaging in discussions, and connecting with like-minded individuals, and this guide will help you make the most of it.

For Those Curious About Social Media Trends

Lastly, if you're someone curious about how social media works or the role X plays in shaping public discourse, this book offers valuable insights. You'll gain a deeper understanding of the platform's unique culture, its impact on society, and the opportunities it presents for individuals and organizations alike.

What You'll Gain From This Book

Regardless of your background, goals, or experience level, this book is designed to provide you with practical, actionable knowledge. By the end of this guide, you'll have the skills and confidence to navigate X effectively, whether you're using it for personal, professional, or business purposes.

1.3 How to Use This Guide

Welcome to **"Social Media X (Twitter): Everything You Need to Know to Get Started."** Whether you are completely new to X (formerly known as Twitter) or have some experience but want to maximize your impact, this guide is designed to be a **comprehensive, step-by-step resource** that helps you navigate and master the platform.

What You Can Expect from This Book

This book is structured in a way that allows you to **progress from beginner to advanced user** at your own pace. Each chapter covers essential aspects of using X, from setting up your profile to growing your audience, engaging effectively, and even monetizing your presence.

Here's a quick breakdown of what you'll find:

- **Introduction:** This section provides background on X and explains why it's a valuable platform for personal and professional use. It also outlines who will benefit most from this book.

- **Chapter 1: Getting Started with X (Twitter):** A hands-on guide for setting up your account, understanding the platform's interface, and learning the essential features.

- **Subsequent Chapters:** More advanced topics such as engagement strategies, content creation, advertising, monetization, and security best practices.

Each chapter is structured with **clear explanations, practical examples, and actionable steps** so you can apply what you learn immediately.

How to Read This Guide

There are two primary ways to use this book:

1. **Step-by-Step Learning Approach** – If you are new to X, it's best to read the book sequentially. This will allow you to build a **solid foundation** before moving on to more advanced topics.

2. **Quick Reference Guide** – If you already have experience with X and are looking for specific insights, you can jump to the relevant chapters or sections. Each section

is designed to be **standalone**, meaning you can find actionable advice without having to read everything before it.

Icons and Special Formatting

To make this guide easy to follow, we use the following formatting:

- **Key Takeaways:** At the end of each major section, you'll find a quick summary of the most important points.

- **Pro Tips:** Highlighted advice and best practices from experienced X users.

- **Common Mistakes:** Warnings about pitfalls and errors to avoid.

- **Step-by-Step Instructions:** Whenever a process is involved (e.g., setting up your profile), it will be presented in a numbered format for easy execution.

- **Real-World Examples:** Case studies and real-life tweets from individuals and brands that illustrate key points.

Who Should Use This Guide?

This book is written for a **broad audience**, including:

- **New Users:** If you've never used X before, this guide will walk you through every step of getting started.

- **Casual Users:** If you have an account but aren't sure how to use X effectively, this book will help you become more confident.

- **Business Owners and Entrepreneurs:** Learn how to use X for branding, customer engagement, and marketing.

- **Content Creators and Influencers:** Discover strategies for growing an audience and monetizing your presence.

- **Professionals and Job Seekers:** Find out how to build a strong online presence for networking and career growth.

No matter what your goals are, this guide provides **practical insights** that you can use to make the most of X.

How to Get the Most Out of This Book

To fully benefit from this book, consider the following:

1. **Apply What You Learn Immediately** – The best way to learn is by doing. As you read, take action by setting up your account, optimizing your profile, and experimenting with different features.

2. **Engage with the X Community** – Follow influencers, industry leaders, and communities that align with your interests. Interaction is key to success on X.

3. **Stay Updated on Platform Changes** – Social media platforms evolve frequently. While this guide covers fundamental strategies, always be open to learning about new features and updates.

4. **Experiment and Analyze Results** – What works for one user might not work for another. Try different engagement tactics, content formats, and posting schedules to see what resonates with your audience.

5. **Take Notes and Reflect** – Keep a journal of what works for you. Which tweets get the most engagement? What times do your followers respond best? Reviewing your progress will help you refine your approach.

A Roadmap for Success on X (Twitter)

To help you track your learning, here's a suggested roadmap for implementing what you learn from this book:

Week 1: Getting Started

- Sign up for an account if you haven't already.

- Set up your profile with a strong bio, profile picture, and header.

- Familiarize yourself with the X interface (home feed, explore, notifications).

- Follow at least 20 accounts in your industry or interest area.

Week 2: Posting and Engagement

- Create your first **tweet** and use a **relevant hashtag**.

- Reply to at least **five tweets** from other users to engage in conversations.

- Experiment with **retweeting and quote tweeting**.

- Test different **tweet formats** (text-only, images, GIFs, polls).

Week 3: Growing Your Presence

- Start a **content schedule** (e.g., post once per day).

- Try writing a **thread** to share insights or tell a story.

- Join discussions using **popular hashtags** in your industry.

- Identify **engaging accounts** and interact consistently.

Week 4: Advanced Features and Optimization

- Explore **Twitter Spaces** (join or host a discussion).

- Create **lists** to organize your feed.

- Analyze your **tweet performance** using Twitter analytics.

- Adjust your strategy based on what's working.

By following this structured approach, you'll be able to **build confidence, gain followers, and use X effectively** for personal or professional growth.

Final Thoughts

This book is designed to **empower you with the knowledge and tools needed to navigate X (Twitter) effectively**. Whether you're here to **connect, share, build a brand, or grow an audience**, this guide will help you achieve your goals in a clear, step-by-step manner.

Now that you know how to use this book, let's move on to **Chapter 1**, where we'll dive into setting up your X (Twitter) account and optimizing your profile for success.

Key Takeaways:

✓ This book is structured for **both beginners and experienced users**, allowing for step-by-step learning or quick reference.

✓ It includes **practical tips, real-world examples, and actionable steps** to help you implement strategies immediately.

✓ Success on X requires **consistent engagement, experimentation, and adapting to platform changes**.

✓ Follow the suggested **four-week roadmap** to gradually build your presence and expertise on X.

Are you ready to begin your journey on X? Let's get started with **Chapter 1: Getting Started with X (Twitter)!**

CHAPTER I
Getting Started with X (Twitter)

2.1 Creating Your Account

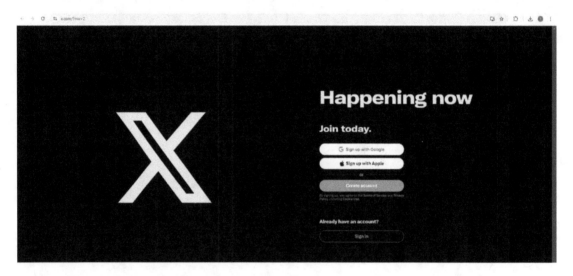

Getting started on X (formerly known as Twitter) is easy, and in this section, we will guide you through every step necessary to set up your account and get ready to dive into the world of social media. Whether you're joining for personal use, to connect with others, or to grow your business, this section will ensure that you're fully equipped with all the knowledge you need.

Why Create an Account on X (Twitter)?

Before diving into the process of setting up your account, let's understand why you might want to join X in the first place. X offers a platform to share your thoughts, connect with others, stay updated on trending topics, and discover new content. It's an excellent place to engage with influencers, brands, and communities or simply follow your favorite celebrities, politicians, or businesses.

X allows for real-time information sharing, so whether you're looking to network, market your business, or simply have conversations, this social media platform is a great option. Once you understand why X is important to you, let's proceed with the steps to create your account.

Creating Your X Account

Once you've settled on a username, you can proceed with creating your account. Let's break down the process step by step:

Option 1: Creating a New Account on X (Twitter)

1. **Download the App or Visit the Website**: Go to your mobile app store (Google Play or the App Store) and download the official X app. Alternatively, you can visit the X website at www.twitter.com.

2. **Click on "Sign Up"**: When you open the app or website, click on the "Sign Up" button to begin creating a new account. On the app, this is typically displayed clearly on the main screen.

3. **Enter Your Details**: You will be prompted to enter basic information, including your name, phone number, or email address.

   o **Name:** This is your display name, which will appear on your profile. You can use your real name or a business name here.

   o **Phone Number or Email:** You can choose either phone number or email to create an account. Make sure the email is valid and accessible, as you'll need it for account verification and recovery.

4. **Set Your Password**: Choose a strong and secure password. It's important to use a combination of letters, numbers, and symbols to make your password hard to guess. X recommends using a password that is at least 8 characters long.

5. **Customize Your Account (Optional)**: X will offer the option to import contacts from your phone or email to find people you already know. You can skip this step if you prefer to search for accounts manually later.

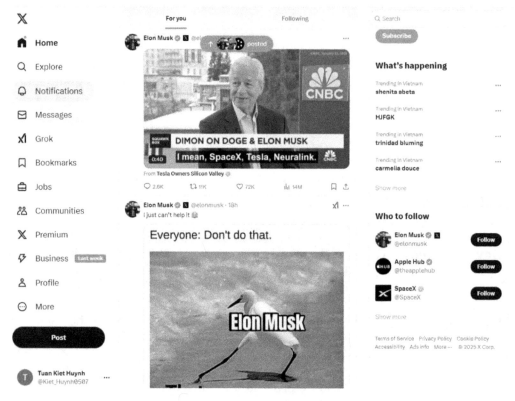

2.1.1 Choosing the Right Username (@Handle)

Choosing the right username for your X (formerly Twitter) account is one of the most important steps in building your online presence. Your username, also known as your @handle, is the first thing people will notice when they come across your profile. It's how people will tag, mention, and identify you on the platform. Having a memorable and well-chosen username can make a significant difference in your engagement and overall visibility. Here's a detailed guide to help you choose the best username for your X account.

Why Is Your Username Important?

Before diving into how to pick a username, let's first understand why your username is so important.

1. **Brand Identity**: Your username is an essential part of your brand identity, whether it's personal or business-related. It should represent you or your brand accurately

and be easy to recall. For businesses, it's an opportunity to stay consistent with the brand name you use across other platforms.

2. **Recognition and Discoverability**: A good username can enhance your discoverability on X. When users search for your name, a relevant and unique username makes it easier for them to find you. A memorable @handle can lead to higher engagement because people are more likely to remember you and tag you in their posts.

3. **Professionalism and Credibility**: A username that aligns with your goals, whether personal or professional, adds credibility. For personal accounts, it helps present your online persona. For businesses, it's crucial to appear professional and approachable to your audience.

4. **First Impressions**: Your username is the first impression you give to potential followers. If it's easy to understand and relates to your interests or business, it makes people more likely to follow you and engage with your content.

Things to Consider When Choosing a Username

Now that we understand the importance of your username, let's break down the key factors to consider when selecting your @handle.

1. Keep It Short and Simple

One of the key characteristics of a good username is simplicity. The best usernames are often short, simple, and easy to remember. Avoid long, complicated usernames that can be hard to spell or type. People should be able to remember your username after seeing it once.

For example, instead of something like @SuperAwesomePersonWhoLovesCats, consider @AwesomeCatLover or something that conveys your personality or interests in a clear and succinct way.

Pro Tip: If your desired username is too long, try using initials, acronyms, or shortening words to make it more concise. You can also use symbols like underscores to break up long names. However, keep in mind that too many symbols can make your username difficult to remember.

2. Be Unique and Stand Out

While it's important to keep your username simple, it's equally important to ensure it's unique. The more distinctive your username, the more likely it is to be noticed. Avoid generic names or ones that are too similar to others.

A unique username helps you stand out and be easily identifiable. For example, instead of using something like @JohnSmith, consider incorporating your niche, personality, or a fun twist that reflects who you are. For instance, @UrbanExplorerJohn could stand out more if you're a travel or adventure enthusiast.

Pro Tip: If the username you want is already taken, try variations such as adding your profession, hobby, or location. You can also add a number (but avoid using random numbers, as they don't add meaning) or underscores to differentiate yourself.

3. Reflect Your Brand or Personality

Your username should reflect who you are or what your brand represents. For personal accounts, think about what defines you—whether it's your passion for cooking, your expertise in technology, or your love for fitness. Your username should give new visitors an instant idea of what you're all about.

For businesses, your username should ideally align with your business name or what you offer. If you run a clothing store, a username like @TrendyThreads could reflect your business identity.

If you're using X for professional networking or business purposes, it's best to choose a username that maintains a level of professionalism. Avoid using slang, emojis, or anything too casual that could make you look unprofessional in the eyes of potential clients or colleagues.

4. Make It Easy to Spell and Pronounce

Another key factor to keep in mind when choosing your username is how easy it is to spell and pronounce. If you have a complicated username, people may struggle to find you or tag you correctly. A simple username is easier for your followers to share with others and refer to in conversation.

Pro Tip: When choosing your username, say it out loud to yourself and to others. If it's easy to say and doesn't sound confusing when spoken, it's likely easy to remember and spell as well.

5. Avoid Using Too Many Numbers or Special Characters

While numbers or special characters may help differentiate a taken username, they can also complicate things. If your username includes a string of random numbers or symbols, it can become harder for people to recall and search for.

Numbers can be particularly problematic because they don't have a meaningful context unless they're relevant to you (e.g., a birth year or a product name). Special characters such as dashes or underscores can also cause confusion, as some users may forget them or not know they're part of your username.

Instead, focus on creating a meaningful and simple username without relying on numbers or symbols.

Additional Tips for Choosing Your Username

1. Consistency Across Platforms

If you plan to build a personal brand or business presence on multiple social media platforms, consistency is key. Try to choose a username that is available on other platforms like Instagram, Facebook, and LinkedIn. This helps you maintain a unified online presence, making it easier for people to find and connect with you.

2. Think About Your Long-Term Goals

When picking your username, consider your long-term goals. If you want to build a personal brand, you may want to select a username that reflects your personal identity and can grow with you as your career or interests evolve. For businesses, consistency with your brand name or a clear reflection of your products/services is essential for recognition.

3. Check for Availability

Before you get too attached to a username, check if it's available. X has a search function that allows you to check if your desired username is already taken. If the username you want is unavailable, think of alternatives or be creative with variations while keeping it simple and on-brand.

Pro Tip: If your username is taken by someone else, don't feel discouraged. Try adding a descriptive word related to your niche or profession to make it unique. Just make sure it still aligns with your brand.

4. Future-Proof Your Username

As your brand or presence grows, you may expand to other platforms or evolve your focus. Choose a username that's flexible and not too narrowly defined. For example, if you are a fitness coach, instead of using something like @YogaQueen, you might opt for @FitWithJenna or @CoachJenna to keep things broader and more versatile.

Conclusion: Your Username is Your Identity

Choosing the right username on X is an essential step in your social media journey. A memorable, simple, and unique @handle can help you stand out, increase your discoverability, and enhance your credibility. It's not just about being recognized—your username represents who you are, your brand, and the community you're building. Take your time, be thoughtful, and don't be afraid to experiment with different ideas. Remember, once you've chosen a great username, you're one step closer to establishing your presence and starting your journey on X.

2.1.2 Setting Up Your Profile (Bio, Profile Picture, Banner)

Your X (Twitter) profile is your first opportunity to make a lasting impression. Whether you are using the platform for personal use, as a business, or to build your professional brand, having a well-crafted profile can help you stand out. In this section, we'll guide you through setting up your bio, profile picture, and banner, making sure that each component reflects who you are and aligns with your goals.

1. Profile Picture: Creating a Memorable First Impression

Your profile picture is the first thing people see when they visit your profile or when they come across your tweets in their timeline. This image is a crucial part of your personal brand, so it's essential to choose a high-quality, representative photo. Let's dive into how you can select and upload the best profile picture for your X (Twitter) account.

Choosing the Right Profile Picture

- **Professional vs. Personal:** The type of profile picture you choose should align with the purpose of your X account. If you are using your account for personal reasons, a casual photo of yourself will work. However, for business or professional purposes, opt for a clear, high-quality image that shows your face and conveys professionalism. A business logo works best for a brand or company page.

- **Quality Over Quantity:** The image should be of high resolution and clear, without any distractions or unnecessary clutter in the background. Ensure your face or brand logo is easily visible, even when the image is reduced to a smaller size.

- **Consistency Across Platforms:** If you are using X to promote your personal or business brand, try to maintain consistency across all your social media profiles by using the same profile picture. This helps your audience quickly recognize you across different platforms.

- **Lighting and Composition:** For personal profiles, good lighting can make a significant difference. Avoid harsh lighting that creates shadows. Natural light works well, especially when taken outdoors. If possible, avoid selfies that may appear too casual or low quality. For business profiles, a clean, well-lit photo of your logo or company symbol works best.

Uploading Your Profile Picture

To upload your profile picture, follow these simple steps:

1. **Open X (Twitter) and go to your Profile:** Click on your profile icon in the top left of the home screen.

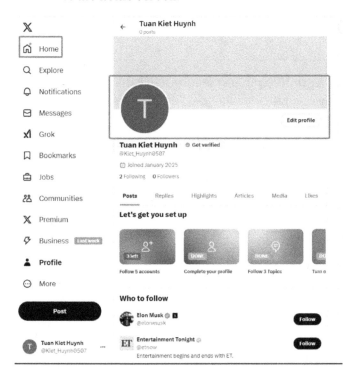

2. **Edit Profile:** Click the "Edit Profile" button on your profile page.

3. **Upload Your Picture:** Under the profile picture section, click on the camera icon. Choose an image file from your computer or device. The image should be square (the recommended dimensions are 400x400 pixels).

4. **Adjust and Crop:** After selecting the image, you can crop it to fit the frame. Ensure your face or logo is centered and visible.

5. **Save Changes:** Once you are satisfied with your image, click "Save" to update your profile.

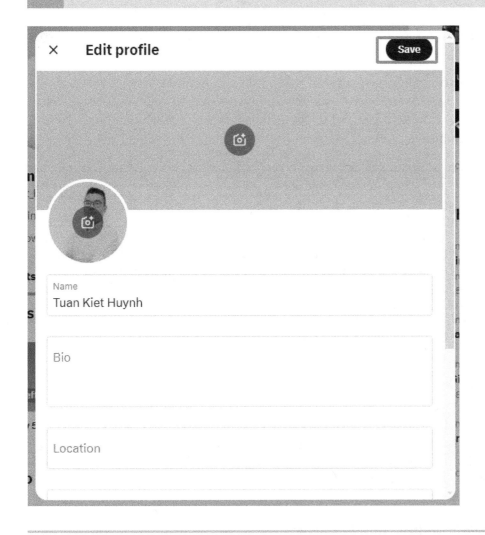

2. Profile Bio: Crafting the Perfect Introduction

Your bio is a concise introduction to who you are or what your brand represents. It appears right below your profile picture, and this small section is essential for engaging potential followers. Whether you are an individual or business, your bio should communicate your value proposition clearly and effectively.

Writing Your Bio

- **Be Clear and Concise:** You only have 160 characters in your bio, so make every word count. Include key information that reflects who you are and what your profile represents. Think about what makes you or your brand unique and highlight that in a succinct manner.

- **Use Keywords and Hashtags:** If you want to increase your discoverability, consider using relevant keywords or hashtags related to your niche or industry. For example, a marketing expert might include terms like #DigitalMarketing, #SEO, or #ContentStrategy.

- **Include Your Interests or Services:** If you're an individual, you can mention your personal interests, hobbies, or professions. A business might describe the services it provides, its core values, or a call to action, such as "DM for inquiries" or "Visit our website for more details."

- **Show Personality:** Don't be afraid to let your personality shine through your bio. Whether you choose to add humor, a quote, or a unique fact, this section should give people a reason to follow you and engage with your content.

- **Use Emojis Sparingly:** Emojis can help break up text and make your bio more visually appealing. However, don't overuse them. Choose emojis that align with your message and avoid making your bio look cluttered or difficult to read.

Tips for Writing a Strong Bio

Here are some tips to make your bio more effective:

- **Use a Call to Action:** If you want people to take specific action after visiting your profile (like following you, visiting your website, or checking out your blog), include a clear call to action. For example, "Follow for daily tips" or "Click below to learn more."

- **Link to Your Website or Other Socials:** If you are a business or influencer, include a link to your website, portfolio, or other social media accounts to encourage cross-platform engagement.

- **Add a Touch of Humor or Creativity:** Depending on your personality, you can incorporate a little bit of humor or wit into your bio to make it memorable.

Examples of Strong X (Twitter) Bios

- **Personal Profile:** "Digital marketer | Coffee lover | Travel addict | Helping brands grow online. Let's connect! ☕✈️🗺 #MarketingTips"

- **Business Profile:** "Award-winning bakery serving the best cupcakes in town 🍰 | Order now! | DM for custom orders ☐ #BakingWithLove"

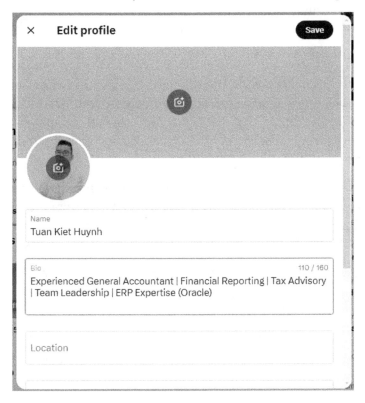

Updating Your Bio

To update your bio, follow these steps:

1. **Go to Your Profile:** Click on your profile icon in the top left corner.

2. **Edit Profile:** Click on the "Edit Profile" button.

3. **Update Bio:** In the "Bio" section, delete or edit your current bio to reflect any changes.

4. **Save Changes:** Once you're happy with the update, click "Save" to apply the changes.

3. Profile Banner: Customizing Your Background

Your profile banner is the large header image at the top of your profile. This image can be used to further showcase your personal or business identity and create a more visually appealing profile. It offers additional space to be creative and is often the first thing users notice when they land on your page.

Choosing the Right Banner Image

- **Reflect Your Brand Identity:** For businesses, the banner image should reflect the company's ethos, products, or services. This could be an image of your products, office space, or a promotional graphic that ties into your current campaigns. Personal accounts might opt for a landscape photo, a creative shot, or something that aligns with their interests.

- **High-Quality Image:** Just like your profile picture, your banner image should be high quality. Low-resolution images can make your profile look unprofessional and unappealing. Aim for an image that's at least 1500x500 pixels to ensure it appears crisp and clear.

- **Keep It Simple and Clean:** Avoid cluttering your banner with too much text or imagery. Focus on creating a clean, visually striking image that conveys your message clearly without overwhelming visitors.

- **Align with Your Bio:** If you're using your profile to promote a business, product, or cause, make sure your banner image complements the bio and provides a consistent message about who you are or what you offer.

Uploading Your Banner Image

Here's how to upload or change your banner image:

1. **Go to Your Profile:** Click on your profile icon in the top left.

2. **Edit Profile:** Click on the "Edit Profile" button.

3. **Upload Banner Image:** Click on the camera icon located at the top of the banner section. Choose an image from your device and upload it.

4. **Adjust and Crop:** If needed, crop or adjust the image so that it fits correctly within the banner space.

5. **Save Changes:** Once you're satisfied with the banner, click "Save" to apply the changes.

Tuan Kiet Huynh ✓ Get verified
@Kiet_Huynh0507

Experienced General Accountant | Financial Reporting | Tax Advisory | Team Leadership | ERP Expertise (Oracle)

📅 Joined January 2025

2 Following   **0** Followers

4. Final Thoughts on Profile Customization

Your profile on X (Twitter) is a direct reflection of you or your brand. Taking the time to carefully craft your bio, choose a professional profile picture, and upload a visually appealing banner image can make a significant impact on how others perceive you. By following these steps and best practices, you'll set yourself up for success and start building a strong presence on the platform.

Remember, consistency is key! Keep your profile updated and in line with your personal or business goals.

2.1.3 Understanding Privacy and Security Settings

When creating an account on X (Twitter), ensuring that your privacy and security settings are properly configured is vital. In a world where online privacy is increasingly important, especially on a global platform like X, taking control of these settings can help protect your personal information, prevent unwanted interactions, and manage your digital footprint. Let's walk through the essential privacy and security settings and explain how to configure them to safeguard your account.

1. Privacy Settings Overview

Privacy settings on X allow you to control who can see your content and interact with you. By default, your tweets are public, meaning anyone can view them, like, retweet, or reply to them. However, you can modify your privacy settings to make your account more secure, private, and personal.

Protect Your Tweets

One of the first things you may want to do when setting up your privacy settings is to consider whether to make your tweets private or public. The default setting is public, meaning anyone—whether they are following you or not—can see what you post.

If you decide to protect your tweets, only people you approve as followers will be able to view your posts. Here's how to enable this setting:

1. Go to your **Settings and Privacy** menu by clicking on your profile icon in the top left corner.

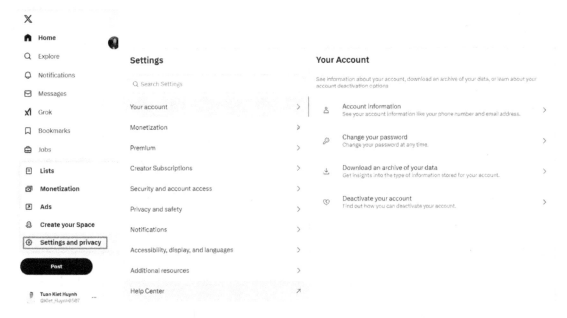

2. Navigate to **Privacy and Safety**.

3. Under the **Audience and Tagging** section, toggle the option to **Protect your Tweets**.

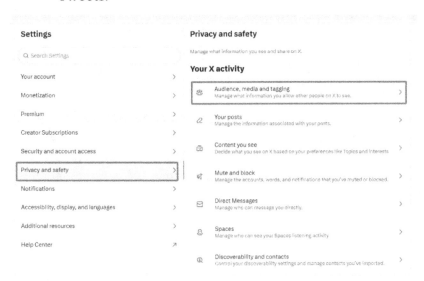

4. Once enabled, a small lock icon will appear next to your username, signifying that your tweets are private.

← **Audience, media and tagging**

Manage what information you allow other people on X to see.

Protect your posts ☐
When selected, your posts and other account information are only visible to people who follow you. Learn more

Protect your videos ☐
If selected, videos in your posts will not be downloadable by default. This setting applies to posts going forward and is not retroactive Learn more

Photo tagging ＞
Anyone can tag you

Who Can See Your Tweets

Even with protected tweets, it's important to know who has access to your posts. X offers settings that allow you to control who can see and interact with your tweets in more granular ways:

- **Public (unprotected tweets)**: Anyone, including people who don't follow you, can see your tweets.

- **Followers Only (protected tweets)**: Only people you approve as followers will see your tweets.

You can always change these settings later by visiting your privacy settings. Note that protecting your tweets also restricts your visibility in search results outside X.

Managing Followers

When you protect your tweets, only approved followers can see your posts. But what if you have followers you no longer trust or want to interact with? X allows you to manage your followers by removing them from your followers list. This means they can no longer view your protected tweets, but they can still see your public tweets.

To manage your followers:

1. Visit your profile.

2. Click on your **Followers** list.

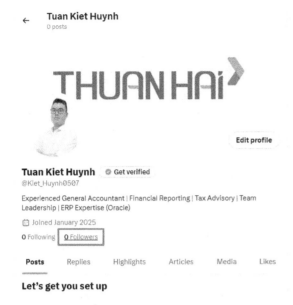

3. Find the follower you wish to remove, click the three-dot icon beside their name, and select **Remove Follower**.

This option is useful for maintaining your privacy without blocking users completely.

2. Managing Interactions

Privacy on X extends beyond who can see your content; it also involves who can interact with you. The platform offers several settings to control who can reply, mention, or message you.

Who Can Reply to Your Tweets

If you want to limit who can reply to your tweets, you can change the settings on each tweet you post. By default, everyone can reply, but you can customize this for each tweet:

1. When composing a tweet, click on the **globe icon** to the left of the **Tweet** button.

2. Choose one of the following options:

   o **Everyone**: Anyone can reply to your tweet.

   o **People You Follow**: Only people you follow can reply.

   o **Only People You Mention**: Only those you tag in the tweet can reply.

This feature helps you manage conversations and avoid unwanted responses.

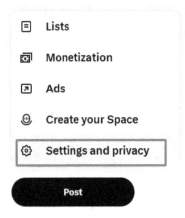

Mentioning You in Tweets

If you don't want people to mention you in their tweets, you can adjust this in your settings. By default, anyone can mention you in their tweets, but you can restrict it:

1. Go to **Settings and Privacy**.

2. Navigate to **Privacy and Safety**.

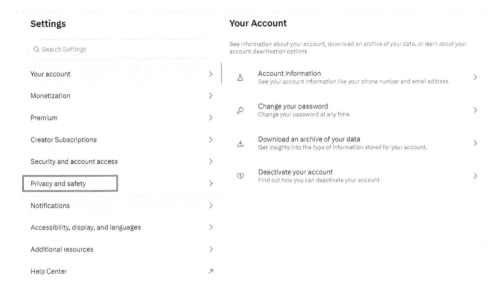

3. Under **Photo tagging**, choose the option that suits you best:

    o   **Everyone**: Anyone can mention you.

    o   **People You Follow**: Only people you follow can mention you.

    o   **Only People You Follow You**: Only users you follow and who follow you back can mention you.

This setting is crucial for maintaining a more controlled and secure social media experience.

← **Photo tagging**

Photo tagging

Allow people to tag you in their photos and receive notifications when they do so.

Anyone can tag you

Only people you follow can tag you

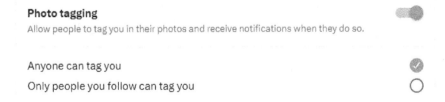

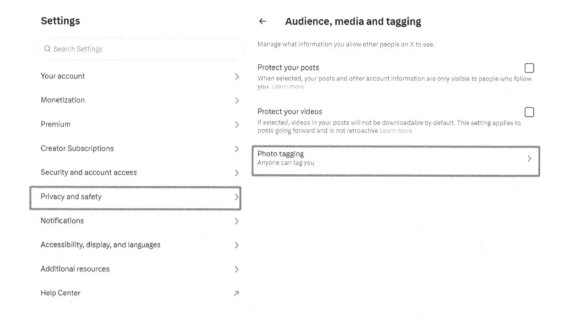

Direct Messages (DMs)

Direct messaging on X allows users to privately communicate with one another. By default, anyone can send you a direct message. However, you may prefer to limit this feature to only people you follow or who follow you.

To manage who can send you DMs:

1. Go to **Settings and Privacy**.

2. Navigate to **Privacy and Safety**.

3. Under **Direct Messages**, toggle the option to allow **Anyone to Message You** or **Only People You Follow**.

By restricting direct messages, you can avoid unsolicited messages from people you don't know or don't trust.

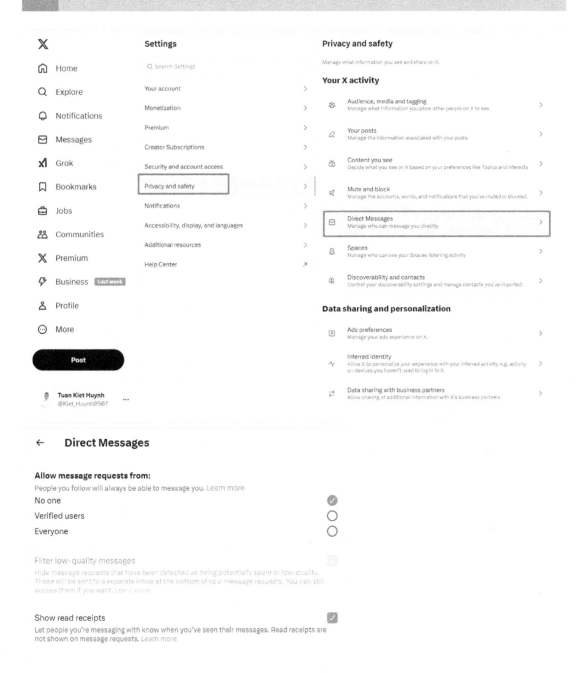

3. Security Settings Overview

Security settings are just as important as privacy settings, as they protect your account from unauthorized access and hacking attempts. Here are the critical security features X offers to secure your account.

Enabling Two-Factor Authentication (2FA)

Two-factor authentication (2FA) is one of the most important steps you can take to protect your account from hackers. With 2FA enabled, you'll need to enter a code sent to your mobile device or email whenever you log into X from a new device or location.

Here's how to set up 2FA on X:

1. Go to **Settings and Privacy**.

2. Navigate to **Security and Account Access**.

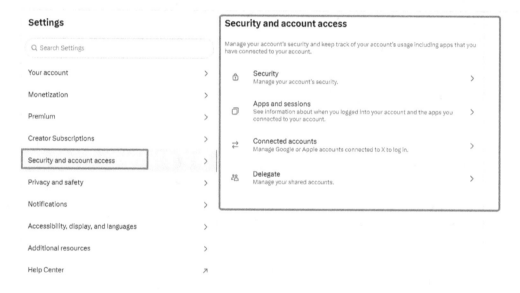

3. Click on **Security** and then **Two-Factor Authentication**.

←   Security

Manage your account's security.

Two-factor authentication

Two-factor authentication   >

Help protect your account from unauthorized access by requiring a second authentication
method in addition to your X password. You can choose a text message, authentication app, or
security key. Learn more

ID verification

ID verification   >

Upload an approved form of identification to confirm the authenticity of your account. Your
information will only be used to validate your identity and will be handled safely and securely.
Learn more

Additional password protection

Password reset protect   ☐

For added protection, you'll need to confirm your email address or phone number to reset your
X password. Learn more

4. You'll be prompted to choose your preferred method of authentication:

    o **Text Message (SMS)**: A code will be sent to your mobile phone via SMS.

    o **Authentication App**: Use an app like Google Authenticator or Authy to generate the authentication code.

    o **Security Key**: If you have a physical security key, you can use it for authentication.

Follow the instructions to set up your selected method, and always keep your backup codes in a secure location in case you lose access to your 2FA method.

Password Management

It's essential to have a strong, unique password to protect your X account. Using a mix of letters (uppercase and lowercase), numbers, and symbols will make your password more difficult to guess.

To change your password:

1. Go to **Settings and Privacy**.

2. Navigate to **Account** and select **Change Password**.

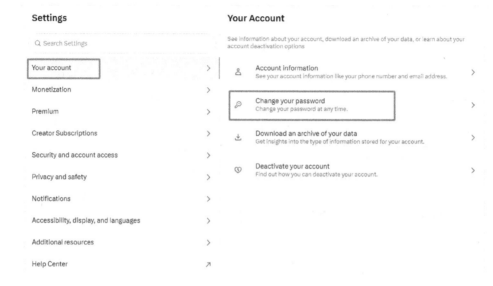

3. Enter your current password and choose a new, secure one.

Make sure to use a password that you haven't used on other platforms and consider using a password manager to help generate and store strong passwords.

App Permissions and Third-Party Access

X allows third-party applications to access your account, but it's essential to review and revoke access to any apps you no longer use or trust. To manage third-party apps:

1. Go to **Settings and Privacy**.

2. Navigate to **Security and Account Access**.

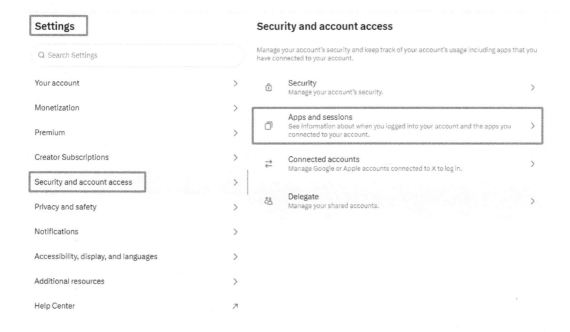

3. Select **Apps and Sessions**, then review the apps connected to your account.

4. Revoke access to any apps you no longer want to use.

←   **Apps and sessions**

See information about when you logged into your account and the apps you connected to your account.

> Connected apps   >

> Sessions   >

> Account access history   >

> Logged-in devices and apps   >

This is especially important if you've used third-party services for tasks like scheduling tweets or automating actions, as they can pose a security risk if compromised.

4. Tracking Account Activity

X offers the ability to track activity related to your account. If you're concerned about unauthorized access, this can be a useful tool to monitor login locations and devices that have accessed your account.

To view recent login activity:

1. Go to **Settings and Privacy**.

2. Navigate to **Security and Account Access**.

3. Under **Apps and Sessions**, click on **Sessions**.

4. You will see a list of all active sessions and devices that have logged into your account.

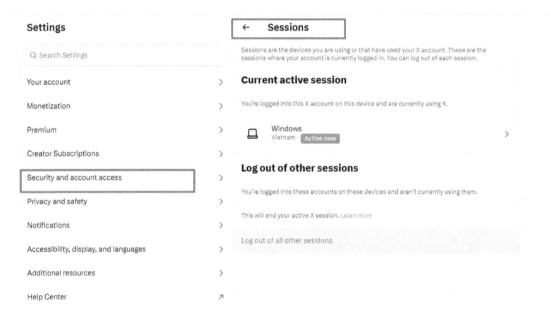

If you notice anything suspicious, you can log out of any unfamiliar sessions to secure your account.

5. Deactivating or Deleting Your Account

If at any point you decide to leave X, you can deactivate your account. Deactivating means your account will be temporarily disabled, but your data will be preserved. If you wish to delete your account permanently:

1. Go to **Settings and Privacy**.

2. Navigate to **Your Account**.

3. Select **Deactivate Your Account** to deactivate it or **Delete Your Account** if you're certain you want to permanently remove it.

Be sure to back up any important data before deleting your account, as all your tweets, media, and followers will be lost permanently.

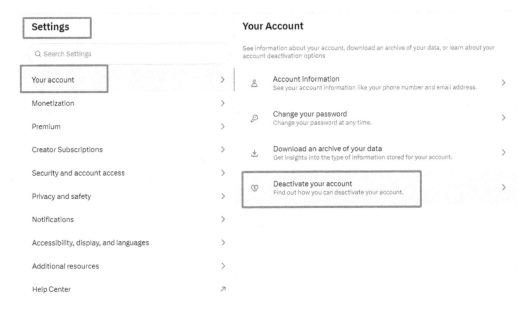

Conclusion

Your privacy and security settings on X are critical for maintaining control over your account and your personal information. By understanding the various privacy and security options available, you can ensure that your social media experience remains safe and aligned with your preferences. Take the time to regularly review these settings and stay informed about any updates X may make to improve the security of its platform.

2.2 Navigating the X (Twitter) Interface

2.2.1 Home Feed and Timeline

When you first log into X (formerly Twitter), the **Home Feed** (or **Timeline**) is the primary screen you'll encounter. This feed is a dynamic stream of tweets from accounts you follow, along with tweets that are tailored to your interests. Navigating this feed is essential for getting the most out of X. It serves as your gateway to interaction, engagement, and discovery on the platform. Let's break down the key elements that make up the Home Feed, how it works, and how to effectively use it.

Understanding the Home Feed

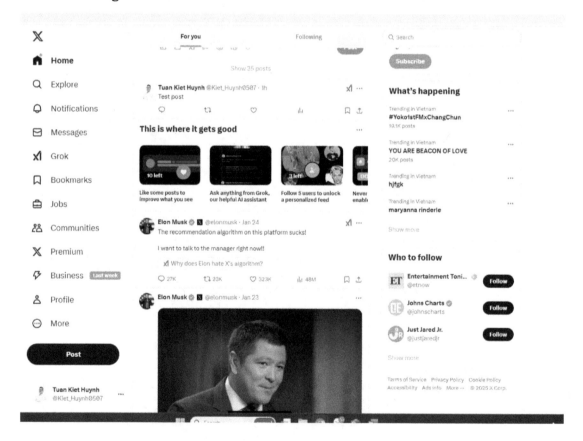

The Home Feed is a continuously updated stream of content that includes tweets, retweets, media, and replies. It is important to recognize that the Home Feed is personalized to each user based on various factors. Unlike static social media platforms, X is designed to bring you real-time content, making your feed feel fresh and continuously engaging. Here's how the Home Feed functions:

- **Tweets from Followed Accounts**: The majority of your Home Feed consists of tweets from people, organizations, and brands you follow. You'll see their posts appear in reverse chronological order unless X's algorithm decides to promote certain tweets.

- **Promoted Tweets**: Sponsored content will appear in your feed, marked with the word "Promoted." These tweets are advertisements from businesses or influencers who are paying to have their content shown to a specific audience.

- **Trending Topics**: Based on your location and interests, X may show you trending topics or hashtags. These can be seen at the top of the feed or under the Explore tab. Engaging with these trends can help you expand your reach and discover relevant content.

- **Tweets You Might Like**: X uses machine learning to suggest tweets that you might enjoy, based on your interactions, followed accounts, and search history. This section of the feed provides a mix of organic content that you haven't directly followed but may find interesting.

How the Home Feed is Organized

The Home Feed is built to keep you engaged for as long as possible. X uses several elements to keep you hooked, such as notifications, retweets, and replies. But to truly understand how the feed works, it's important to distinguish between different types of content that appear in your timeline.

Tweets

- These are individual posts made by users. Tweets can include plain text, images, GIFs, videos, links, or polls. The character limit for a tweet is 280 characters, which allows users to share short, concise thoughts or pieces of content.

- Tweets can be retweeted, liked, or replied to, and each of these actions impacts how the tweet appears in your feed. Tweets with more engagement (likes, replies, retweets) may be promoted by X's algorithm as part of your feed to encourage interaction.

Retweets

- When you see something on your feed that you find interesting or entertaining, you can retweet it to share it with your followers. Retweets help spread content and increase the visibility of tweets. Retweeting can be done with or without adding your own comment (known as a "quote tweet").

- **Quote Tweets**: When you add your own thoughts along with the original tweet, this is called a quote tweet. These tweets can add context, humor, or opinion to the content you're sharing. The original tweet appears below your comment, and followers can engage with both your post and the original tweet.

Replies

- Replies are responses to tweets, either from the original poster or from anyone else. Conversations on X often happen via replies, with a series of back-and-forth exchanges taking place under a tweet. Replies are an excellent way to engage directly with content that interests you.

- A unique feature in the Home Feed is the ability to "expand" a tweet to show all the replies. This allows for more interaction, especially in the case of popular tweets that generate many comments.

Media (Images, GIFs, Videos)

- Media makes your feed more engaging by providing visual content. Tweets that contain images, GIFs, or videos tend to get higher engagement than text-only tweets. This is because media is easier to consume and often more attention-grabbing.

- **Images**: You can add images to your tweets, and they will appear in the feed as a preview. Clicking on the image opens it in full size.

- **GIFs**: GIFs (Graphics Interchange Format) are short, looping animations that are often used to add humor or express emotions. Adding a GIF to your tweet can increase its chances of being retweeted or liked.

- **Videos**: X allows users to upload videos, which can play directly in the feed. Videos are a more immersive form of content, and if done right, they can boost engagement significantly.

Interacting with the Home Feed

The Home Feed isn't just about viewing content—it's also about engagement. Here are the main ways to interact with tweets and users on X:

Liking Tweets

- Liking a tweet is one of the simplest ways to interact. Liking serves as a way to acknowledge the tweet, show your support, or mark it for later viewing. When you like a tweet, the poster will see that you've liked it, and this may lead to more interaction.

- Likes are also visible to your followers, which can spark curiosity and encourage them to check out the tweet.

Retweeting

- Retweeting, as discussed earlier, allows you to share a tweet with your own followers. This is a great way to spread content you find valuable and show support for the original creator. Retweeting also makes the content visible to others who may not be following the original user.

- Retweeting without a comment can be particularly useful when you want to simply share something without adding your own input.

Replying

- If you want to have a conversation with someone or express a more detailed thought about a tweet, replying is the way to go. You can reply directly to the tweet, and it will appear in the conversation thread. Engaging in replies can build connections with other users, increase visibility, and encourage others to interact with you.

Bookmarking Tweets

- If you come across a tweet that you want to refer back to later but don't want to retweet or like, you can bookmark it. Bookmarked tweets are saved in a private collection, allowing you to easily revisit them at any time.

- This feature is especially useful if you want to save tweets for future reference, such as valuable information, funny content, or tweets that provide inspiration.

How X's Algorithm Affects Your Home Feed

One of the key elements that makes X so engaging is its use of an algorithm that personalizes your feed. This means that not all tweets from accounts you follow will show up in your feed in the order they were posted. The algorithm takes various factors into account when determining which tweets to prioritize, including:

- **Engagement History**: X looks at the tweets you've liked, retweeted, and replied to in the past. If you regularly interact with content from certain accounts or on specific topics, X will prioritize similar content in your feed.

- **Content Relevance**: The algorithm also evaluates the relevance of content. For example, if there's breaking news or a viral trend that aligns with your interests, X might highlight that content.

- **Tweet Recency**: While the algorithm does prioritize engagement, X also values fresh content. Recent tweets are more likely to appear toward the top of your feed.

- **Follower Interactions**: If your followers engage with specific tweets, X may push those tweets to the top of your feed as well, even if you didn't follow the original poster.

Customizing Your Feed

Although X's algorithm plays a significant role in shaping your Home Feed, you also have some control over the content you see. Here's how you can customize your experience:

- **Following and Unfollowing**: If you want to see more of a particular type of content, you can follow relevant accounts. Likewise, unfollowing accounts that no longer provide value can help declutter your feed.

- **Mute and Block**: If you want to stop seeing specific content but don't want to unfollow or block an account, you can mute them. Muting hides their tweets from your feed without alerting the account that you've done so.

- **Tailored Content**: You can also explore specific topics or interests on X. This allows the algorithm to better tailor the content in your feed to what you're interested in.

Engagement Tips for Maximizing Your Experience

- **Interact Regularly**: The more you engage with content (like, retweet, reply), the more relevant content X will show you.

- **Follow Influencers and Trending Topics**: Follow industry leaders, celebrities, and trending hashtags to keep your feed full of interesting and timely content.

- **Use Lists to Organize**: If you follow a lot of people, using Lists can help you organize accounts into categories, allowing for more streamlined engagement.

Conclusion

The Home Feed on X (Twitter) is the heart of the platform, where most of your interaction and discovery will take place. By understanding how the feed works, how content is ranked, and how you can engage, you can maximize your experience and use X more effectively. Whether you're looking to engage with friends, follow breaking news, or grow your personal or business brand, the Home Feed is where it all happens. By actively participating in the feed, you can ensure that you stay connected, informed, and engaged in the X community.

2.2.2 Explore Tab: Finding Trends and Topics

The **Explore Tab** on X (Twitter) is a powerful tool that allows you to stay updated on the latest news, trending topics, and conversations happening across the platform. It offers a personalized experience based on your interests, geographic location, and interactions. Understanding how to use the Explore tab can help you stay informed, discover new content, and actively participate in ongoing conversations. In this section, we'll guide you step-by-step on how to effectively navigate the Explore tab and leverage its features to find trends and topics that matter most to you.

1. Accessing the Explore Tab

To begin, it's important to understand how to access the Explore tab on X (Twitter). The Explore tab is a central feature of the platform, and you can easily reach it in just a few taps or clicks, depending on your device.

- **On Desktop**: On the left-hand menu of the X (Twitter) homepage, you'll see an icon resembling a magnifying glass. This is the Explore tab. Simply click on it to enter the Explore section.

- **On Mobile**: On the X mobile app, the Explore tab is represented by the same magnifying glass icon located at the bottom of the screen. Tap it to open the Explore feed.

Once you're in the Explore tab, you'll be greeted with a variety of content, including trending topics, hashtags, news, and tweets related to topics that X (Twitter) believes might interest you.

2. Trending Topics: A Quick Overview

One of the most important features of the Explore tab is the **Trending Topics** section. This section displays a real-time list of hashtags and topics that are currently gaining traction on the platform. Trending topics are curated based on a number of factors, such as the volume of tweets, interactions, and mentions within a certain period.

Understanding Trends

Trending topics are typically shown as a list of hashtags or phrases accompanied by the number of tweets associated with each topic. These trends can change rapidly, so staying on top of them can give you insight into what's happening in the world at any given moment.

- **Worldwide Trends**: These trends reflect topics that are popular globally, allowing you to keep up with what's happening on a global scale.

- **Local Trends**: X (Twitter) also curates trends based on your location, giving you a more localized perspective on what's being discussed in your area or country.

How Trends are Determined

The trends you see are influenced by a combination of factors:

- **Volume of Tweets**: The number of tweets associated with a specific topic or hashtag. The more tweets a topic receives in a short amount of time, the more likely it is to trend.

- **Geographic Location**: Trends are often tailored to your specific location. For example, if a major event is happening in your city, you might see it appear as a trending topic in your Explore feed.

- **Engagement**: High levels of engagement—such as retweets, likes, and replies— also contribute to a topic's trending status.

- **Personal Interests**: Based on the accounts you follow, the topics you engage with, and your past activity, X (Twitter) customizes the trends you see to match your preferences.

Customizing Your Trending Topics

To make sure the trending topics you see are relevant to your interests, X (Twitter) uses an algorithm that tracks the content you engage with. However, if you prefer to see trends that are more closely related to specific areas or subjects, you can adjust your settings:

- **Location Settings**: You can manually change your location settings to view trends specific to different regions. This is useful if you're traveling or if you want to follow trends in other parts of the world.

- **Topic Interests**: X (Twitter) also allows you to follow certain topics, such as sports, politics, or entertainment, so that these topics are prioritized in your trends section.

3. Exploring Specific Trends

Once you've accessed the trending section, you can explore the topics further to gain deeper insights. Clicking on a trending topic will take you to a feed of tweets related to that topic. This feed is dynamic, showing the most recent tweets as well as popular tweets that have received a high level of engagement.

Hashtags and How They Work

Hashtags play a crucial role in helping people find and engage with specific trends. When a topic begins to trend, users often add hashtags to their tweets to make them discoverable by a wider audience. For example, during major events like sports competitions, you might see hashtags like #SuperBowl or #Oscars trending on X (Twitter). Clicking on a hashtag will lead you to a stream of tweets that are discussing that particular topic, making it easy for you to participate in conversations and share your thoughts.

Top Tweets vs. Latest Tweets

In the Explore tab, you'll often be given the option to switch between viewing **Top Tweets** and **Latest Tweets** for a specific trending topic.

- **Top Tweets**: This view shows the most popular tweets, based on engagement metrics such as retweets, likes, and replies. These tweets are typically from well-known accounts or those that have gone viral within the topic.

- **Latest Tweets**: This view presents the most recent tweets related to the trend. It's a great way to stay up-to-date with the latest conversations and discover fresh content in real time.

Engaging with Trends

Once you've explored a specific trend, you can actively participate by liking, retweeting, or replying to tweets within the topic. By engaging with these tweets, you not only join the conversation but also increase the visibility of the topic to your followers.

- **Tweeting Your Thoughts**: Share your opinion or thoughts about the trending topic by creating your own tweet with the relevant hashtag. This can help your voice get heard in larger, ongoing conversations.

- **Retweeting**: Retweet content from others that you find interesting or relevant. This can be an easy way to add your voice to the trend without having to create original content.

- **Replies and Conversations**: Dive into ongoing conversations by replying to tweets and engaging with others in the trend. You can use this as an opportunity to network or share your expertise.

4. Following Trends and Topics That Interest You

If you want to keep track of specific topics over time, X (Twitter) offers the option to follow certain trends or hashtags. By doing so, you can receive notifications and updates whenever these topics are mentioned or discussed on the platform.

Following Hashtags

To follow a specific hashtag, simply click on it in the Explore tab, and then click on the "Follow" button at the top of the page. This will add the hashtag to your list of followed topics, and you'll be notified whenever new tweets with that hashtag appear.

Creating and Following Lists

If you have particular interests, you can also use X's **Lists** feature to create a curated group of accounts or topics related to your interests. For example, you could create a list for **sports news**, **tech updates**, or **political discussions**, and follow the latest tweets from those accounts directly in your feed.

5. Tips for Using the Explore Tab Effectively

To make the most out of your experience in the Explore tab, consider these tips:

- **Be Curious**: Don't just stick to the same trends. Explore new topics and hashtags to expand your knowledge and network.

- **Engage in Real-Time**: Trending topics can change quickly, so engage with content while it's still fresh and relevant. This can increase the likelihood of your tweet being noticed.

- **Use Lists for Personalization**: If you're interested in specific areas, use lists to help filter out irrelevant content and focus on topics that matter most to you.

- **Set Notifications**: For important trends, set up notifications to stay updated in real time.

Conclusion

The Explore tab on X (Twitter) is an invaluable tool for discovering the latest trends, news, and conversations on the platform. By understanding how to use it effectively, you can stay informed, engage with trending topics, and join important discussions. Whether you're using X (Twitter) for personal interests or to enhance your business or brand, the Explore tab allows you to stay relevant and connected to the pulse of the internet.

2.2.3 Notifications and Messages

On X (Twitter), notifications and messages are essential for keeping you engaged with the people, content, and conversations that matter most to you. Understanding how these work will help you stay informed about interactions on your account and maintain control over the types of updates you receive. In this section, we'll dive deep into notifications and messages, guiding you through their features, settings, and strategies for effectively managing them.

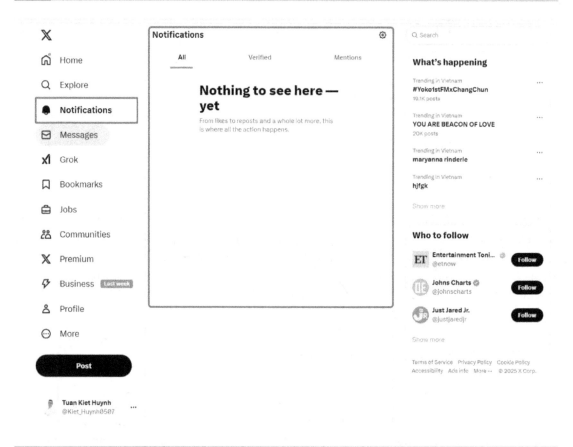

Notifications Overview

Notifications are alerts that notify you about activities on your account, such as mentions, likes, retweets, follows, and interactions in direct messages (DMs). These alerts can come in various forms: pop-up notifications on your device, email alerts, and in-app notifications.

When you first start using X (Twitter), the default settings might bombard you with updates from anyone who interacts with your content. However, it's important to personalize your notification settings to avoid overwhelming yourself with information. By managing your notifications well, you can ensure you're staying connected to the most important conversations and events.

Types of Notifications

Notifications on X (Twitter) are broken down into various categories:

- **Mentions:** When someone mentions your username (@handle) in a tweet, you'll receive a notification. This is one of the most common notifications you'll get and indicates someone is talking about you directly.

- **Likes:** Whenever someone likes your tweet, you'll receive a notification. This shows appreciation for your content and helps you gauge what your audience enjoys.

- **Retweets:** When a user retweets your content, it means they're sharing your tweet with their followers. Retweets are a form of endorsement, and notifications about them can be an important sign of your content's reach.

- **New Followers:** If someone follows your account, you'll be notified. This is a great opportunity to engage with new users and grow your community.

- **Replies:** If someone responds to your tweet, you'll receive a notification of their reply. Engaging with replies is a key part of conversation on X (Twitter), so this notification is essential for keeping the dialogue flowing.

- **Messages (Direct Messages or DMs):** Notifications for DMs let you know when someone is sending you a private message. This is a one-on-one communication feature that is useful for conversations you want to keep away from public view.

- **Trends and News Alerts:** Occasionally, X (Twitter) may push notifications regarding breaking news, trending topics, or events that are generating high user engagement. You can choose to enable or disable these notifications based on your interests.

Managing Your Notifications

X (Twitter) offers customizable settings so that you can control the types of notifications you receive. Here's how you can manage them:

1. **Accessing Notification Settings:**

   o Open X (Twitter) and navigate to the *Settings and Privacy* section of your profile.

   o Tap on the *Notifications* tab. Here, you will see several options to adjust the settings for the different types of notifications.

2. **Customizing Notification Preferences:**

   o **Push Notifications:** These are the notifications that pop up on your device when something significant happens on your account (like a new follower or mention). You can choose which events trigger these notifications and how you receive them (e.g., sound, vibration, or silent).

   o **Email Notifications:** X (Twitter) also allows you to receive email notifications for key activities. You can toggle these on or off, depending on how you want to receive updates.

   o **SMS Notifications:** You can opt to receive text messages for certain actions, such as important account updates or security alerts.

   o **Notification Frequency:** For users who don't want to be overwhelmed, X (Twitter) allows you to control how often you receive notifications. You can choose instant alerts or opt for a daily summary to keep things less intrusive.

3. **Filtering and Prioritizing Notifications:**

   o X (Twitter) allows you to mute notifications from specific users or topics that you don't want to see. For example, if you're following a hashtag that generates too many notifications, you can mute it.

   o You can also prioritize certain types of interactions, ensuring you don't miss important notifications, such as replies from followers or notifications from verified accounts.

Using Direct Messages (DMs) on X (Twitter)

Direct messages (DMs) on X (Twitter) are private conversations between users. This feature is great for private discussions, building relationships with followers, and resolving customer service queries. Here's how to navigate and optimize DMs:

1. **Sending and Receiving DMs:**

   o To send a direct message, simply click on the envelope icon in the top menu of the X (Twitter) app. You'll see a list of conversations you've had, or you can search for someone's username to initiate a new message.

o DMs allow for text-based communication, but you can also send images, GIFs, and videos, making it more versatile for sharing content directly with your contacts.

2. **Managing DM Settings:**

   o **Who Can Message You:** By default, only users you follow can send you DMs. However, you can allow anyone to message you in the settings if you prefer to receive DMs from all users.

   o **Group DMs:** X (Twitter) also supports group direct messages, allowing multiple users to converse together in a private chat. This can be great for collaborations, private events, or just casual conversations.

   o **Message Requests:** If someone who you don't follow tries to DM you, their message will appear in a *Message Requests* folder. This helps you avoid spam or unwanted messages while still giving you control over who can reach you.

3. **Mute and Block in DMs:**

   o If you're receiving unwanted messages or spam, you can mute notifications for that conversation or even block the user. Blocking a user will prevent them from sending you any more DMs or interacting with your content in any way.

4. **Important Considerations for Business Accounts:**

   o For businesses or public figures using X (Twitter), DMs are often an essential tool for handling customer inquiries or responding to direct requests. Managing DMs effectively is vital to maintaining a positive online presence. It's important to have a prompt response time and keep messages professional.

   o Use automated responses to handle common inquiries or direct users to customer service channels.

Best Practices for Notifications and DMs

Notifications and DMs are powerful tools for engaging with your audience on X (Twitter). To make the most of them, follow these best practices:

- **Respond Promptly:** If you receive a mention or reply that requires a response, engage with it quickly. Prompt responses show that you value your audience and are committed to maintaining an active presence.

- **Don't Overwhelm Yourself:** It's easy to get overwhelmed with too many notifications. Use the customization options to ensure you only receive updates that matter to you.

- **Use DMs Wisely:** If you're a business, make sure your DMs are open for customer service and inquiries, but be selective about how and when you respond to avoid becoming overwhelmed.

- **Personalize Your Replies:** Whether it's a DM or a reply to a tweet, adding a personal touch can go a long way. Acknowledge the individual who has interacted with you, and show that you're paying attention to their input.

- **Mute Unwanted Notifications:** If you're receiving notifications for things that aren't useful, mute them. For instance, if a specific hashtag or topic is generating too much noise, muting it will allow you to focus on what's important.

Summary

Notifications and messages are at the heart of interaction on X (Twitter). Understanding how to manage these features effectively will help you stay connected with the right people, track important conversations, and ensure that your engagement with others is meaningful. By customizing your notifications and utilizing direct messages wisely, you can control your social media experience and stay focused on what matters most.

2.2.4 Settings and Customization

Once you've created your account and explored the main features of X (Twitter), it's time to dive deeper into the settings and customization options that help you personalize your experience. X (Twitter) offers a wide array of tools and settings that allow you to tailor the platform to your specific needs and preferences. In this section, we will cover the key aspects of X's settings, from privacy control to notification preferences, and guide you through the process of making the platform work for you.

1. Accessing Settings on X (Twitter)

To begin customizing your X (Twitter) experience, you first need to access the settings menu. Here's how to find it:

- **Desktop (Web Browser)**:
    - On your desktop, go to X and log into your account.
    - In the sidebar on the left, click on your profile picture or the "More" option (three dots).
    - Scroll down and click on **Settings and privacy**. This will take you to a screen with various categories, including Account settings, Privacy settings, and more.

- **Mobile (X App)**:
    - Open the X app on your smartphone or tablet.
    - Tap on your profile icon or the navigation menu in the top left corner.
    - Scroll down to **Settings and privacy** and tap to open the settings menu.

Once you're in the settings menu, you can explore the different sections to customize how you use X (Twitter).

2. Privacy and Safety Settings

One of the most important areas of customization on X (Twitter) is privacy. X provides you with control over who can see your tweets, interact with you, and find your account. Here are some critical privacy settings you should review:

Protect Your Tweets

By default, your tweets are public and visible to anyone who visits your profile or searches for content related to your posts. However, you can protect your tweets to make them visible only to your followers. To do this:

- Go to **Settings and privacy** > **Privacy and safety** > **Audience and tagging**.
- Toggle the **Protect your Tweets** option on. This means only people who follow you can see your posts, and new followers must be approved.

Block and Mute Accounts

Sometimes, you may come across individuals whose interactions you do not wish to engage with. X allows you to block or mute users, both of which limit their ability to interact with your content.

- **Blocking**: If you block someone, they won't be able to follow you, see your tweets, or interact with you in any way. To block someone, go to their profile, click the three dots (More options), and select **Block**.

- **Muting**: Muting an account allows you to keep following them while hiding their tweets from your feed. Muting is perfect if you don't want to block someone outright but don't want to see their posts. To mute an account, go to their profile, click the three dots, and select **Mute**.

Settings

Q Search Settings

Your account	>
Monetization	>
Premium	>
Creator Subscriptions	>
Security and account access	>
Privacy and safety	>
Notifications	>
Accessibility, display, and languages	>
Additional resources	>
Help Center	↗

Privacy and safety

Manage what information you see and share on X.

Your X activity

Audience, media and tagging
Manage what information you allow other people on X to see. >

Your posts
Manage the information associated with your posts. >

Content you see
Decide what you see on X based on your preferences like Topics and interests >

Mute and block
Manage the accounts, words, and notifications that you've muted or blocked. >

Direct Messages
Manage who can message you directly. >

Spaces
Manage who can see your Spaces listening activity >

Discoverability and contacts
Control your discoverability settings and manage contacts you've imported. >

← **Mute and block**

Manage the accounts, words, and notifications that you've muted or blocked.

Blocked accounts	>
Muted accounts	>
Muted words	>
Muted notifications	>

Managing Who Can Tag You

You can control who can tag you in tweets, which helps protect your privacy and control the conversations you're part of. To adjust this setting:

- Go to **Settings and privacy** > **Privacy and safety** > **Audience and tagging**.

- You can choose whether to allow anyone to tag you, only people you follow, or no one at all.

3. Notification Preferences

Notifications on X (Twitter) help you stay updated with important interactions and updates, but sometimes, too many notifications can become overwhelming. X allows you to manage notifications based on various preferences.

Types of Notifications

You can control the types of notifications you receive, such as mentions, retweets, direct messages, and more.

- Go to **Settings and privacy** > **Notifications** > **Push notifications**.

- You'll see several categories like **Mentions, Followers, Likes, Retweets**, etc.

- You can toggle each category on or off based on what you'd like to be notified about.

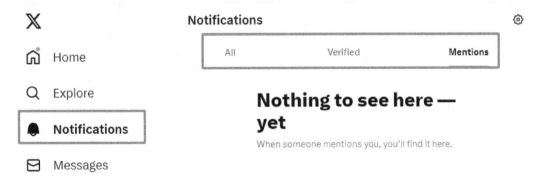

Email Notifications

X also sends email notifications about certain activities like new followers, direct messages, and tweet activity. You can customize this setting to limit email clutter.

- Go to **Settings and privacy** > **Notifications** > **Email notifications**.

- Toggle the settings based on your preferences. For example, you may want to receive emails for direct messages but not for every mention.

Managing Push Notifications

On mobile, push notifications can be a great way to stay updated on your account activity in real time. However, if you're receiving too many notifications, you can fine-tune them:

- Open **Settings and privacy** > **Notifications** > **Push notifications**.

- Adjust which notifications you receive as push alerts on your mobile device.

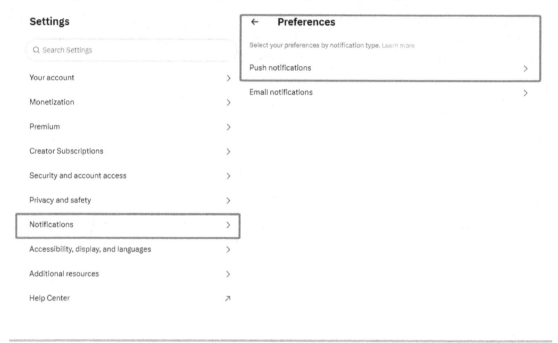

4. Customizing Your Profile and Display

X (Twitter) offers several customization options to help you express your personality or brand through your profile.

Updating Your Profile Picture and Banner

Your profile picture is the first thing others see when they visit your account, so it's essential to choose an image that represents you well. The banner is a large image that appears at the top of your profile page and allows for further expression.

To update both:

- Go to your profile page and click the **Edit profile** button.

- To change your profile picture, click on the profile photo area and upload a new image from your device.

- To change your banner, click on the banner image area and select a new image.

Customizing Your Bio

Your bio is an important part of your profile and should provide others with information about who you are, what you do, or what your account represents. You can use up to 160 characters to describe yourself.

To update your bio:

- Go to **Edit profile** and type in your new bio. Be creative and concise while making sure it aligns with your purpose on the platform.

Choosing a Theme (Light or Dark Mode)

If you're looking for a more personalized and visually comfortable experience, you can choose between light and dark themes for your interface.

- On desktop, go to **Settings and privacy** > **Display** > **Dark Mode**.

- On mobile, go to **Settings and privacy** > **Display and sound** > **Dark Mode**.

Toggle between the two themes based on your preferences, or select **Automatic** to adjust based on the time of day.

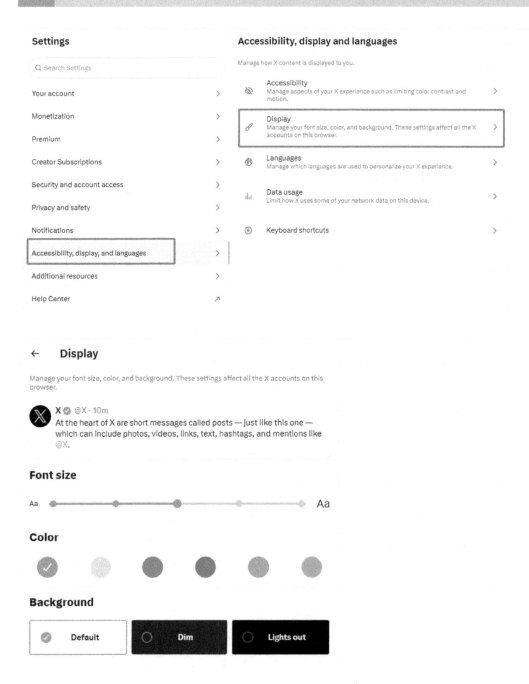

Settings

Q Search Settings

Your account   >

Monetization   >

Premium   >

Creator Subscriptions   >

Security and account access   >

Privacy and safety   >

Notifications   >

Accessibility, display, and languages   >

Additional resources   >

Help Center   ↗

Accessibility, display and languages

Manage how X content is displayed to you.

Accessibility
Manage aspects of your X experience such as limiting color contrast and motion.   >

Display
Manage your font size, color, and background. These settings affect all the X accounts on this browser.   >

Languages
Manage which languages are used to personalize your X experience.   >

Data usage
Limit how X uses some of your network data on this device.   >

Keyboard shortcuts   >

← **Display**

Manage your font size, color, and background. These settings affect all the X accounts on this browser.

X ✔ @X · 10m
At the heart of X are short messages called posts — just like this one — which can include photos, videos, links, text, hashtags, and mentions like @X.

Font size

Aa ●———●———●———●———● Aa

Color

Background

Default   Dim   Lights out

---

5. Account Security and Authentication

Protecting your account is essential, especially with the increased risk of hacking and identity theft on social media platforms. X (Twitter) provides multiple ways to secure your account.

Two-Factor Authentication (2FA)

Enabling 2FA adds an extra layer of security to your account by requiring a second form of verification when you log in.

To enable 2FA:

- Go to **Settings and privacy** > **Security and account access** > **Security** > **Two-Factor Authentication**.

- Choose your preferred 2FA method (text message, authentication app, or security key).

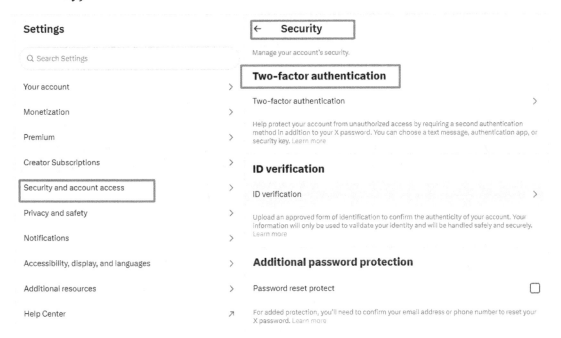

Password Reset and Recovery

If you forget your password or suspect someone has accessed your account without permission, you can reset it easily through your email or phone number.

- Go to the login page and click on **Forgot password?**.

- Enter your email address or phone number, and follow the instructions sent to you.

6. Data Usage and Analytics

X provides users with data analytics to help track performance, such as the number of impressions, engagements, and followers you gain over time.

Twitter Analytics

If you're using X (Twitter) for business or branding, X offers a detailed analytics dashboard. To access it:

- Go to **More** > **Analytics**.

- You'll see insights on your tweets' performance, including engagement rates, impressions, and audience demographics.

By customizing these settings and understanding your data, you can make the most of X (Twitter) for personal use or business goals.

7. Final Thoughts

Customizing your X (Twitter) experience ensures that you enjoy a secure, personalized, and enjoyable time on the platform. Whether you're managing privacy, notifications, or profile elements, X provides a range of tools to make your account truly your own.

CHAPTER II
Understanding X (Twitter) Basics

3.1 How Posting Works

3.1.1 Writing Your First Post (Tweet)

When you're just starting on X (formerly known as Twitter), writing your first post (or tweet) is an exciting moment! Tweets are the core of interaction on X, where you share your thoughts, news, and updates in a short format. But don't worry if you're unsure where to start – this guide will walk you through everything you need to know to craft your first tweet and set yourself up for success on the platform.

Step 1: Understanding the Basics of a Tweet

A tweet on X is a short message that you share with your followers, or anyone who visits your profile. Tweets can contain up to **280 characters**, which may seem like a small amount, but it's plenty of space to share an idea, link, or even engage with others.

Your tweet can also include:

- **Images** (up to 4 images or a single image/video)
- **GIFs** (an animated image)
- **Polls** (to engage your audience with questions)
- **Hashtags** (to categorize content or increase visibility)
- **Links** (to share websites, articles, etc.)
- **Mentions** (to tag others in your tweet)

- **Emojis** (to add personality or visual interest)

Step 2: Structuring Your Tweet

While X (Twitter) is known for brevity, it's important to craft your tweet thoughtfully. Here's a simple structure you can follow:

1. **Opening**: Start with a hook or introduction. This can be a question, statement, or even a thought-provoking comment. The first few words are crucial as they often determine whether someone will engage with your tweet.

Example:

- o "What's your favorite way to stay productive during the week?"

- o "Did you know that Twitter started in 2006?"

2. **Main Content**: This is the heart of your tweet. Here, you can share the core message, opinion, or fact. Be clear and concise with your writing.

Example:

- o "I love using X (Twitter) to stay connected with the latest tech trends. It's such a quick way to stay updated!"

- o "Today marks the 10th anniversary of X (Twitter) – an amazing milestone for the platform!"

3. **Call to Action (Optional)**: If your goal is to engage others, encourage your followers to take action. A call to action could be a question, invitation to reply, or share their thoughts.

Example:

- o "What do you think about the new features on X? Drop your thoughts in the comments below!"

- o "Retweet if you agree that X (Twitter) is the best platform for breaking news."

4. **Hashtags (Optional)**: Hashtags help categorize your tweet and make it discoverable to a wider audience. You can use up to **2-3 hashtags** in each tweet, but avoid overloading your tweet with them. Choose relevant and trending hashtags when possible.

Example:

- o "This is an exciting time for the tech world! #TechTrends #Innovation"
- o "Celebrating the anniversary of X! #HappyBirthdayX"

Step 3: Keeping It Engaging

To capture the attention of your audience, keep your tweet engaging and relatable. Here are some tips to make your tweet stand out:

1. **Be authentic**: Don't try to sound too formal or scripted. Twitter is about personality, so let your true voice shine through.

Example:

- o "Can't wait to grab some coffee this morning! Who's with me? ☕ #MorningVibes"

2. **Ask Questions**: Asking a question encourages engagement and invites people to reply, which increases interaction with your tweet.

Example:

- o "What's one productivity tip you swear by? Share your secrets! #ProductivityHacks"

3. **Use Humor**: If it fits your style, humor is a great way to grab attention. Be mindful of your audience and the tone of the conversation, but don't be afraid to be light-hearted.

Example:

- o "Trying to stay focused today... but Netflix keeps calling me! 😄 #ProcrastinationProblems"

4. **Incorporate Visuals**: Adding an image, GIF, or video to your tweet makes it more visually appealing and likely to grab attention. Tweets with visuals tend to perform better than those without.

Example:

- o Post a picture of your morning coffee with the caption: "Good morning, X! ☕ Ready to tackle the day! #MorningCoffee"

Step 4: Avoiding Common Mistakes

While posting your first tweet is fun, there are a few common mistakes that can hinder your success:

1. **Overcrowding with Hashtags**: While hashtags are useful, too many can make your tweet look spammy. Stick to 1-3 relevant hashtags.

Example:

- Instead of: "Check out the new gadget! #Technology #Gadget #Innovation #Tech #Cool"

- Try: "Check out the new gadget! #TechInnovation"

2. **Forgetting to Proofread**: Double-check your tweet for spelling, grammar, or punctuation errors before posting. A polished tweet reflects well on you and keeps your audience engaged.

3. **Being Too Generic**: Tweets that sound like everyone else's won't stand out. Be sure to share your unique perspective or add value to the conversation.

Example:

- Instead of: "X is great!"

- Try: "I've been using X for 6 months, and it's been a game-changer for staying updated with industry news."

4. **Not Engaging with Others**: Social media is about conversation, so don't forget to respond to comments and engage with your followers. Twitter is a two-way street, and active engagement leads to better relationships and visibility.

Step 5: Publishing Your Tweet

Once you're happy with your tweet, it's time to hit the "Tweet" button! But before you do, here are a few things to consider:

- **Timing**: The timing of your tweet matters. Tweets are more likely to get noticed if you post them when your audience is most active. Check out trending topics or tools that tell you when your followers are online.

- **Audience**: Keep in mind who you're speaking to. Are you tweeting for your business, for fun, or to engage with a specific group? Tailor your tweet to your audience.

- **Tone**: Consider the tone of your tweet. Should it be casual, professional, or funny? A good understanding of your brand or personal tone helps you communicate more effectively.

Once you've clicked **Tweet**, your message is live! Feel free to share your tweet with friends or ask others to retweet it, but remember, the key to success on X (Twitter) is consistency. Keep tweeting, engaging, and evolving your content as you grow your presence.

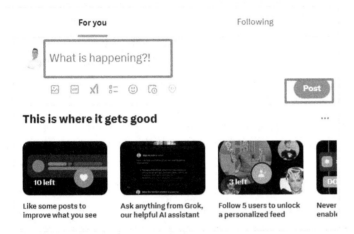

Conclusion

Writing your first tweet is just the beginning of your journey on X (Twitter). It's essential to practice and refine your tweeting skills, understand the nuances of the platform, and develop your unique voice. By following these steps, you'll be able to make a strong first impression and start building meaningful interactions with your audience.

3.1.2 Using Hashtags Effectively

Hashtags are one of the most powerful tools on X (Twitter), enabling users to categorize their content, increase discoverability, and engage with a larger audience. Whether you're a beginner looking to increase your reach or an experienced user wanting to fine-tune your strategy, understanding how to use hashtags effectively can significantly boost your presence and engagement on the platform. In this section, we'll explore the fundamentals of hashtags, their importance, and how you can strategically use them to grow your audience and enhance the effectiveness of your posts.

What Are Hashtags?

At its core, a hashtag is simply a word or phrase preceded by the pound symbol (#). When used in a post, hashtags serve as a clickable link that directs users to a feed of tweets containing the same hashtag. This functionality allows people to discover content related to specific topics, trends, or conversations. Hashtags can be used for a variety of purposes, from joining a trending topic to promoting a brand or cause.

Why Are Hashtags Important on X (Twitter)?

1. **Increased Visibility**: Hashtags help your tweet get discovered by people who are interested in the topics you're discussing. By using popular or relevant hashtags, your content is included in the public conversation and can be seen by a larger audience, even those who don't follow you yet.

2. **Categorization of Content**: Hashtags allow you to categorize your content into topics, making it easier for users to find tweets on specific subjects. This is especially helpful if you're sharing information or opinions on a particular event, industry, or interest area.

3. **Joining Trending Conversations**: On X (Twitter), trending hashtags are a reflection of what's happening in real-time. By participating in these conversations using trending hashtags, you can get involved with a much larger community of people and become part of a global discussion.

4. **Branding and Campaigns**: Hashtags can be used to promote your brand or specific marketing campaigns. Custom hashtags related to your business, product, or service can help create a sense of community and encourage user-generated content.

5. **Improved Engagement**: Hashtags improve engagement by allowing users to find and interact with content that resonates with their interests. Tweets with relevant hashtags tend to receive more likes, retweets, and replies because they're more discoverable.

Choosing the Right Hashtags

Not all hashtags are created equal, and choosing the right ones is critical to your success on X (Twitter). Here are some key considerations when selecting hashtags for your tweets:

1. **Relevance**
   The most important aspect of choosing a hashtag is ensuring it's relevant to your content. Using hashtags that don't relate to your tweet may confuse or irritate users and may not result in meaningful engagement. For example, if you're sharing a post about a new product launch, using a general hashtag like #love may not bring the attention you need, whereas a hashtag like #newproductlaunch or #techinnovation would attract a more targeted audience.

2. **Popular vs. Niche Hashtags**: There are two main types of hashtags to consider:

   o **Popular Hashtags**: These are widely used and often trend on the platform. While using them can give you immediate visibility, they're also highly competitive, meaning your tweet might get lost in a flood of content. For instance, hashtags like #MondayMotivation or #TechNews are popular but may be too general for niche content.

   o **Niche Hashtags**: These are more specific to a certain interest or community. While they may have a smaller audience, they offer a more engaged and targeted group of users. For example, if you're tweeting about a specific programming language, using hashtags like #JavaScriptDev or #PythonProgramming will connect you with a dedicated group of tech enthusiasts.

3. **Trending Hashtags**: Trending hashtags on X (Twitter) are a goldmine for real-time engagement. When you see a topic trending, it's an opportunity to join a large conversation. However, it's essential that your tweet adds value to the conversation. Simply adding a trending hashtag to a tweet without context might seem inauthentic or spammy. Ensure your tweet is relevant and thoughtful when participating in trending discussions.

4. **Brand-Specific Hashtags**: Custom hashtags that are unique to your brand, event, or campaign help build recognition and a sense of community. For example, if you're launching a new product, you can create a hashtag such as #ProductNameLaunch. Encouraging your followers to use your branded hashtag makes it easier to track conversations and engage with your audience.

5. **Hashtag Length and Clarity**: While it's tempting to use multiple words in a single hashtag, it's essential to keep hashtags concise and clear. Long hashtags can be hard

to read and may confuse users. Additionally, overly complex hashtags may result in typos or misspellings. For maximum impact, try to keep your hashtags short and to the point while still conveying the essence of your message.

How Many Hashtags Should You Use?

The number of hashtags you use in a tweet can significantly affect your post's performance. While X (Twitter) allows you to add as many hashtags as you want, research suggests that using **1 to 3 hashtags** per tweet is optimal for engagement. Here's why:

1. **Quality Over Quantity**: Using too many hashtags can overwhelm your audience and make your tweet look cluttered. A tweet with too many hashtags may also appear less authentic or professional. Instead, choose the most relevant hashtags to avoid overloading your followers with unnecessary information.

2. **Engagement Declines with Excessive Hashtags**: According to studies, tweets with **more than two hashtags** tend to experience a decrease in engagement. This suggests that using too many hashtags dilutes the focus of the message and reduces the likelihood that users will engage with the content.

3. **Focus on the Most Impactful Hashtags**: Prioritize hashtags that will help you reach the right audience. Focus on a few powerful and well-researched hashtags rather than stuffing your tweet with many generic ones.

Best Practices for Using Hashtags

1. **Do Your Research**: Before using a hashtag, take the time to research its popularity and relevance. There are several tools available that can help you find trending hashtags, such as Twitter's own trending topics, or third-party tools like Hashtagify or RiteTag. Researching hashtags will also help you avoid using hashtags that have been co-opted by negative or controversial content.

2. **Monitor Hashtags for Performance**: Track how your tweets perform when you use specific hashtags. You can use X (Twitter) analytics to monitor engagement rates on posts with hashtags and adjust your strategy based on the results. If a particular hashtag is yielding a higher engagement rate, you may want to use it more often.

3. **Experiment with Hashtags**: Don't be afraid to experiment with different types of hashtags. Mix and match popular, niche, and branded hashtags to see which ones resonate most with your audience. Over time, you'll learn which hashtags work best for your specific content and audience.

4. **Don't Overload Your Tweets**: As mentioned earlier, using too many hashtags can hurt your tweet's engagement. Stick to a small number of carefully selected hashtags that align with your message and goals. Quality matters more than quantity.

5. **Use Hashtags in Context**: Ensure that your hashtags are used in a way that makes sense within the context of your tweet. Avoid the temptation to use hashtags just for the sake of gaining visibility. Your audience will appreciate authentic and relevant content more than generic or spammy posts.

Examples of Effective Hashtag Usage

Here are a few examples of how you can effectively use hashtags on X (Twitter):

1. **Product Launch Announcement**: "We're excited to announce the launch of our new smartphone! 🚀 #TechInnovation #SmartphoneLaunch #FutureOfTech"

2. **Join a Trending Conversation**: "Supporting climate action today at the global summit! ☐ #ClimateChange #GlobalSummit #ActNow"

3. **Share Industry Insights**: "Did you know? 60% of businesses have shifted to digital marketing this year. 🚀 #DigitalMarketing #MarketingTrends"

4. **Create a Branded Campaign**: "Join our #FitnessJourney challenge and share your progress with us! ☐☐♂☐ #FitnessGoals #GetActiveWithUs"

Conclusion

Hashtags are a crucial component of your X (Twitter) strategy, allowing you to connect with a larger audience, join conversations, and promote your content. By using hashtags effectively, you can increase your visibility, engage with relevant communities, and achieve your social media goals. Remember to keep your hashtags relevant, targeted, and concise. Regularly evaluate your hashtag performance and adjust your approach based on the results. With these strategies in hand, you'll be well on your way to mastering the art of hashtagging on X (Twitter).

Example 1: Product Launch Announcement

Imagine you're launching a new product—a smartphone. Here's how you might use hashtags to increase visibility and engagement:

Tweet: "We're excited to announce the launch of our new smartphone! 🚀 Featuring cutting-edge technology and unbeatable performance. Pre-order now! #TechInnovation #SmartphoneLaunch #FutureOfTech"

Explanation:

- **#TechInnovation** targets users interested in the latest technological advancements, which helps position your smartphone as part of cutting-edge tech.

- **#SmartphoneLaunch** directly relates to the event of launching a new product, making it easier for users looking for product launches to find your tweet.

- **#FutureOfTech** is a broad but relevant hashtag that aligns with users interested in the future of technology, drawing in a larger audience.

Example 2: Joining a Trending Conversation

Let's say there's a global summit on climate change happening, and the hashtag #ClimateChange is trending. You decide to join the conversation with a tweet that supports the event:

Tweet: "Supporting climate action today at the global summit! ☐ It's time to take action and make a difference.
#ClimateChange #GlobalSummit #ActNow"

Explanation:

- **#ClimateChange** is a widely recognized and trending hashtag, connecting your tweet to the ongoing global discussion about climate change.

- **#GlobalSummit** ties the tweet to the specific event, making your message more relevant to those following the summit.

- **#ActNow** encourages urgency and motivates others to take immediate action, aligning with the spirit of the event and adding a sense of call-to-action to your post.

Example 3: Sharing Industry Insights

If you're sharing a statistic or insight about the marketing industry, using hashtags that cater to the marketing community helps you reach people interested in those topics:

Tweet: "Did you know? 60% of businesses have shifted to digital marketing this year. 🚀 Stay ahead with the latest trends in the digital world! #DigitalMarketing #MarketingTrends #BusinessGrowth"

Explanation:

- **#DigitalMarketing** targets a specific audience that's focused on online marketing strategies, making your content more discoverable to professionals in this field.

- **#MarketingTrends** attracts those keeping up with the latest industry changes and trends, increasing the chances that your tweet will resonate with users looking for up-to-date information.

- **#BusinessGrowth** broadens your reach to users interested in improving their business performance and scaling their operations through marketing strategies.

Example 4: Creating a Branded Campaign

Imagine you want to promote a fitness challenge your brand is hosting. Here's how you can use branded hashtags to create a sense of community and encourage user participation:

Tweet: "Join our #FitnessJourney challenge and share your progress with us! □□♂□ Stay motivated and let's get stronger together. #FitnessGoals #GetActiveWithUs"

Explanation:

- **#FitnessJourney** is a custom hashtag created for your specific campaign, allowing participants to easily share their progress and connect with others taking part.

- **#FitnessGoals** is a relevant and widely used hashtag for those interested in setting and achieving fitness goals, linking your challenge to broader fitness discussions.

- **#GetActiveWithUs** is another branded hashtag that encourages users to participate and engage, creating a sense of community around your brand's fitness challenge.

Example 5: Using Niche Hashtags for Specific Content

Let's say you're a developer sharing insights about JavaScript. Using niche hashtags allows you to target a more specific audience of developers:

Tweet: "Excited to dive deeper into JavaScript today! Here's a quick tutorial on how to use asynchronous functions. 💻
#JavaScriptDev #WebDevelopment #CodingTips"

Explanation:

- **#JavaScriptDev** targets developers specifically interested in JavaScript, connecting your content to a highly engaged community of professionals in the field.

- **#WebDevelopment** broadens the scope of your tweet, making it discoverable by people interested in the broader field of web development.

- **#CodingTips** appeals to both beginners and seasoned coders who are looking for valuable coding advice and quick solutions to problems.

Example 6: Leveraging a Local Hashtag for Regional Engagement

If you're hosting a local event or discussing a regional topic, using location-based hashtags can help you reach a targeted audience.

Tweet: "Can't wait for the tech meetup tomorrow in San Francisco! Join us for insightful talks and networking with fellow innovators.
#SFTechMeetup #SanFranciscoEvents #TechCommunity"

Explanation:

- **#SFTechMeetup** is a localized hashtag that focuses specifically on tech events in San Francisco, making it easier for local tech enthusiasts to find and join the conversation.

- **#SanFranciscoEvents** connects your tweet to other events happening in the area, appealing to individuals looking for activities or meetups in the region.

- **#TechCommunity** appeals to a broader tech audience who may not be in San Francisco but are still interested in joining discussions about the tech industry.

Example 7: Engaging in a Trending Topic with Humor

Hashtags don't always need to be serious. You can use trending topics to join light-hearted or humorous conversations. For example, if there's a trending meme about office life:

Tweet: "When your coffee kicks in before your meeting, and you're ready to conquer the day! ☕☕
#MondayMotivation #CoffeeAddict #WorkLife"

Explanation:

- **#MondayMotivation** is a popular and recurring hashtag used to inspire and motivate people, making it the perfect fit for this light-hearted tweet.

- **#CoffeeAddict** targets coffee lovers, using humor to connect with an audience that shares the same love for caffeine.

- **#WorkLife** reflects the everyday experiences of professionals, appealing to anyone who has dealt with similar office scenarios.

Conclusion

These examples highlight the diversity of hashtag usage on X (Twitter). Whether you're joining a trending conversation, sharing industry insights, promoting a personal brand, or simply adding humor to your tweets, hashtags play a pivotal role in expanding your reach and increasing engagement. By understanding how to select the right hashtags, using them strategically, and staying consistent with your approach, you can harness the full potential of hashtags to boost your presence on X (Twitter).

3.1.3 Tagging and Mentioning Others

Tagging and mentioning other users on X (formerly Twitter) is a fundamental feature that enhances engagement, increases visibility, and fosters community interaction. Whether you're participating in conversations, crediting sources, or replying to tweets, knowing how to use tags and mentions effectively can significantly improve your social media experience.

In this section, you'll learn:

- The difference between tagging and mentioning

- How to tag and mention users properly

- Best practices for using mentions without spamming

- How mentions impact engagement and visibility

1. Understanding the Difference: Tagging vs. Mentioning

Although often used interchangeably, **tagging** and **mentioning** have distinct functionalities on X.

- **Mentioning:** When you include another user's **@username** anywhere within a tweet, reply, or comment, you are "mentioning" them. This is commonly used to refer to someone, start a conversation, or give credit.

- **Tagging:** While X (Twitter) does not have a direct "tagging" feature like Instagram or Facebook, the term is sometimes used when users mention others in **tweets, replies, or media posts (such as photos or videos).**

In summary, **all tags are mentions, but not all mentions are considered tags.**

2. How to Mention Someone in a Tweet

Mentioning in a Regular Tweet

To mention someone in a regular tweet, follow these steps:

1. **Compose a new tweet** by clicking on the "+" icon or "Post" button.

2. **Type "@" followed by the person's username** (e.g., @elonmusk).

3. **Select the correct username from the dropdown list** that appears.

4. **Complete your tweet** and click "Post."

Example:
"Had an amazing discussion with @JohnDoe today! Looking forward to our next collaboration."

In this example, @JohnDoe will receive a notification that they have been mentioned.

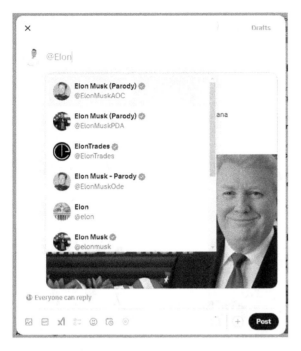

Mentioning Someone in a Reply

Replies are a great way to interact directly with other users. To mention someone in a reply:

1. **Click "Reply"** below a tweet.

2. **Type your message**, and include **"@" followed by the username** of the person you want to mention.

3. **Post the reply**—the mentioned user will receive a notification.

Example:

"Great insights in your last post, @MarketingGuru! I completely agree with your point about engagement strategies."

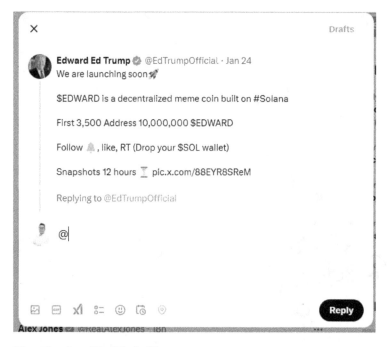

Mentioning Multiple Users

You can mention **multiple users in a single tweet** by including multiple @usernames.

Example:
"Excited for the upcoming event with @TechWorld and @StartupInsider! Who else is attending?"

However, be mindful not to **overuse mentions** in a way that looks like spam.

3. Mentioning Users in Photos and Videos

X allows you to tag users in images, making it easier to credit people or get their attention without using up your tweet's character limit.

How to Tag Users in Photos

1. **Compose a tweet** and attach an image.

2. Click **"Who's in this photo?"** below the image.

3. **Type the usernames** of the people you want to tag.

4. **Select the correct usernames from the list.**

5. **Post the tweet.**

The tagged users will be notified, and others can tap the image to see who is tagged.

Example:
"A fantastic panel discussion today at the tech conference! @JaneDoe @JohnSmith @TechGuru #Tech2025"

Note:

- Users can **adjust their privacy settings** to prevent being tagged in images.

- You can **tag up to 10 people per photo**, and it does **not** count toward the tweet's character limit.

---

4. Best Practices for Tagging and Mentioning

When to Mention Someone

- **To credit content:** If you are sharing someone's article, artwork, or insights, mention them to acknowledge their work.

- **To start a conversation:** Engaging with industry leaders or peers can help you build your presence.

- **To participate in discussions:** Joining conversations using mentions makes your responses more visible.

- **To notify a brand or person:** If you're talking about a company or a well-known figure, mentioning them can increase the chances of engagement.

Example:
"Just read an amazing book on digital marketing by @MarketingExpert! Highly recommend it."

When NOT to Mention Someone

- **Spamming mentions:** Don't mention random people hoping for engagement.

- **Forcing interactions:** Don't mention influencers or celebrities repeatedly if they're not engaging with you.

- **Over-tagging in replies:** If you are responding to a tweet, only mention users relevant to the conversation.

Bad Example:
"@ElonMusk @BillGates @JeffBezos @Oprah @neiltyson Check out my website and retweet!"
This looks like spam and is unlikely to get any engagement.

5. How Mentions Affect Engagement and Visibility

Notifications and Responses

When you mention someone in a tweet, they receive a notification. If they engage (like, retweet, or reply), your post gains **more visibility** due to X's algorithm.

Tip: If you mention someone **without a link**, they are more likely to engage because it doesn't seem promotional.

Algorithm and Reach

Mentioning **active users** can improve your reach since their followers may also see the post. However, if you mention **inactive accounts**, it won't add much value.

The Impact of Verified Mentions

If a **verified** account (with a blue checkmark) interacts with your mention, it can significantly increase your tweet's exposure.

Example:
If a famous entrepreneur replies to your mention, their audience will likely see your tweet, increasing visibility and engagement.

6. Troubleshooting and Managing Mentions

What to Do If Someone Mentions You Unwantedly

If you are mentioned in tweets that you don't want to be part of, you can:

- **Mute the conversation** (so you stop receiving notifications).

- **Block the user** if they continuously mention you in spam posts.

- **Report the tweet** if it's abusive or violates X's policies.

Preventing Yourself from Being Tagged in Photos

If you don't want to be tagged in photos, adjust your settings:

1. **Go to Settings > Privacy and Safety > Photo Tagging.**

2. Select **"Only people you follow can tag you"** or **"Disable photo tagging"** completely.

---

7. Conclusion: Mastering Mentions on X (Twitter)

Tagging and mentioning are essential tools for increasing engagement and building relationships on X. When used correctly, they can:

✓ Enhance networking opportunities

✓ Increase the visibility of your tweets

✓ Encourage meaningful conversations

However, overusing or misusing mentions can **harm your credibility** and annoy your audience. Follow best practices, be mindful of whom you tag, and always engage in a way that adds value to the conversation.

Now that you understand how to tag and mention others effectively, let's move on to the next section: **Liking, Retweeting, and Replying (3.2.1),** where we will discuss how to engage with posts and maximize interaction on X!

3.2 Engaging with Others

3.2.1 Liking, Retweeting, and Replying

Engaging with content on X (Twitter) is one of the best ways to build your presence, interact with others, and grow your network. Among the core engagement features are **Liking, Retweeting, and Replying,** which help users participate in conversations, amplify messages, and express their thoughts. In this section, we'll go into detail about how to use these features effectively, best practices for engagement, and strategies to maximize your impact.

1. Liking Tweets: How and Why to Use the Like Button

What Is the Like Button on X?

The **Like button** (formerly known as the Favorite button) is represented by a **heart-shaped icon** below every post. Clicking this icon allows you to show appreciation for a tweet without having to reply or share it. Liking a tweet serves multiple purposes:

- It lets the author know you appreciate their content.
- It helps **bookmark** tweets you want to return to later.
- It can influence the algorithm, increasing the visibility of certain tweets.
- Other users may see tweets you've liked in their feed (if their algorithm settings allow it).

How to Like a Tweet

To like a tweet, follow these steps:

1. Navigate to a tweet you want to like.
2. Locate the **heart icon** below the tweet.
3. Click or tap the **heart icon**—it will turn red, confirming that you have liked the tweet.
4. To **unlike** a tweet, click the heart again, and it will return to its default state.

Best Practices for Liking Tweets

- Like tweets that genuinely resonate with you—don't just like everything randomly.

- Liking tweets from influencers or industry leaders can help **increase your visibility**.

- Use likes as a **bookmarking tool**—you can access your liked tweets in the **Likes** tab on your profile.

- Be mindful that others can see your liked tweets unless you set your profile to private.

2. Retweeting: Sharing Content with Your Audience

What Is a Retweet?

A **Retweet (RT)** is a way to share someone else's tweet with your followers. When you retweet, the original tweet appears on your profile and timeline, crediting the original author. There are two types of retweets:

1. **Standard Retweet** – Shares the tweet exactly as it is.

2. **Quote Tweet (Retweet with Comment)** – Allows you to add your own thoughts before sharing the original tweet.

How to Retweet a Tweet

To retweet a post, follow these steps:

1. Find the tweet you want to retweet.

2. Click or tap on the **Retweet icon** (two arrows forming a square).

3. Choose one of the following options:

   o **Retweet** (shares the tweet as is).

   o **Quote Tweet** (adds your own comment before retweeting).

4. If you choose **Quote Tweet**, type your message in the box that appears.

5. Click **Post** (or Tweet) to share.

Best Practices for Retweeting

- Retweet valuable content that aligns with your personal or brand image.

- Avoid excessive retweeting without original content—mix in your own tweets.

- Use **Quote Tweets** when you have insights or additional context to add.

- Tag or credit the original author in your Quote Tweet if appropriate.

- Be mindful of **retweeting controversial content**—it can affect how people perceive your profile.

When to Retweet

- When you come across important news, insights, or opinions you want to share.

- If you support a cause, campaign, or announcement.

- To engage with followers by amplifying their content.

- When collaborating with others—retweeting their content builds goodwill.

3. Replying: Engaging in Conversations

What Are Replies on X?

Replies allow you to **directly respond to tweets**, making them a key feature for engagement and interaction. Unlike likes and retweets, replies create a thread, allowing discussions to develop.

How to Reply to a Tweet

To reply to a tweet, follow these steps:

1. Find a tweet you want to respond to.

2. Click or tap the **Reply icon** (speech bubble) below the tweet.

3. A reply box will appear—type your response.

4. Click **Reply** (or Tweet) to send your response.

Alex Jones ✔ @RealAlexJones · 18h

Trump Details Damage From NC Flooding, Announces New Task Force To Fast Track Aid Overriding FEMA and Thanks Elon Musk for Providing Starlink Internet Right After The Storm Saving Lives.

Alex Jones Is Breaking It Down Now:
x.com/i/broadcasts/1...

💬 1.9K   ↻ 19K   ♡ 111K   ᵢₗᵢ 16M   🔖 ⬆

Reply

Best Practices for Replying

- Keep your replies **relevant and respectful**.

- Engage in **meaningful discussions** rather than just replying with generic words like "Great post!"

- If replying to a question, try to provide **value** or helpful information.

- **Use mentions (@username)** to directly engage with people in the conversation.

- Avoid **spammy replies** (e.g., replying with links to promote yourself without context).

Why Replies Matter for Engagement

- Replies create **conversations** and increase visibility.

- They show **you're active and engaged** with your community.

- Consistently replying to industry leaders or influencers **increases your chances of being noticed**.

- Replies can help drive more **traffic to your profile** if others find your responses valuable.

How to Make Your Replies Stand Out

- Be **witty or insightful**—clever replies often get more engagement.

- Use **GIFs, emojis, or images** to make your reply visually appealing.

- Keep your tone conversational and **friendly, even when debating a topic**.

- If you're replying to a long thread, summarize your thoughts clearly.

4. Combining Likes, Retweets, and Replies for Maximum Engagement

To get the most out of your X (Twitter) experience, you should use **all three engagement features together** strategically:

1. **Like** tweets that interest you to **support and bookmark content**.

2. **Retweet** important posts to **share valuable insights** with your audience.

3. **Reply** to tweets to **engage in discussions and build relationships**.

Example Engagement Strategy

- Like tweets from influencers and industry leaders.

- Reply with a valuable comment to start a conversation.

- Retweet insightful tweets and add your thoughts as a Quote Tweet.

How Engagement Helps You Grow

- The more you engage, the **more visible you become** on the platform.

- Engaging in **conversations with the right people** can expand your network.

- Thoughtful replies and retweets position you as **an active, knowledgeable user**.

5. Final Thoughts

Liking, Retweeting, and Replying are **the foundation of engagement on X (Twitter)**. They allow you to participate in discussions, share insights, and build relationships with others. When used strategically, these tools **help you grow your audience, establish credibility, and increase your influence on the platform**.

To master engagement:

✅ Like content that aligns with your interests and values.
✅ Retweet valuable posts to amplify messages.
✅ Reply thoughtfully to foster meaningful conversations.

By consistently engaging in a **genuine and strategic way**, you'll see your presence on X (Twitter) grow, helping you connect with more people and expand your reach.

3.2.2 Quote Tweets vs. Retweets

When engaging with content on X (formerly Twitter), users have multiple options to share and interact with posts. Two of the most important features for content amplification and engagement are **Retweets** and **Quote Tweets**. While they may seem similar at first glance, they serve distinct purposes and can be used strategically to maximize engagement and influence on the platform.

In this section, we will explore the differences between Retweets and Quote Tweets, their best use cases, and strategies for leveraging them effectively.

1. Understanding Retweets and Quote Tweets

Both Retweets and Quote Tweets allow users to share content from others with their followers. However, their functionalities and impact on engagement differ.

What Is a Retweet?

A **Retweet** is a direct re-sharing of someone else's post without adding any personal commentary. When you Retweet a post:

- The original content appears **exactly as it was posted** by the original user.

- The Retweeted post **shows up in your followers' feeds** under your name.

- Your username appears on the Retweet, but you **do not add any additional text to it.**

How to Retweet a Post:

1. Find the post (Tweet) you want to share.

2. Click the **Retweet** icon (a circular arrow symbol).

3. Select **"Retweet"** from the options.

4. The Tweet will instantly be shared with your followers.

What Is a Quote Tweet?

A **Quote Tweet** is similar to a Retweet but allows the user to **add their own commentary** before sharing. Instead of simply reposting the original content, a Quote Tweet enables you to provide **context, opinions, or additional insights**.

How to Quote Tweet a Post:

1. Find the Tweet you want to share.

2. Click the **Retweet** icon.

3. Select **"Quote Tweet"** instead of "Retweet."

4. A text box will appear where you can add your thoughts before sharing.

5. Once you've added your comment, click **"Post"** to share.

Key Differences Between Retweets and Quote Tweets

Feature	Retweet	Quote Tweet
Additional Commentary	No	Yes
Appears as Original Tweet	Yes	No (Appears as a new post)
Boosts Original Post's Engagement	Yes	Yes (but adds a new layer of engagement)
Ideal for	Sharing content quickly	Adding opinions, context, or discussions
Can Start a New Conversation?	No	Yes

2. When to Use Retweets vs. Quote Tweets

Understanding when to use each feature can help you build better engagement and contribute more meaningfully to discussions.

When to Use a Retweet

A **Retweet** is best used when you want to simply amplify a message without adding personal input. Some scenarios where a Retweet is more effective include:

- **Sharing Important News:** If a verified source posts an urgent update, Retweeting ensures it reaches your audience without modification.

- **Supporting a Cause:** If a charity or campaign is promoting an initiative, a Retweet spreads their message without changing their words.

- **Highlighting a Great Post:** When someone posts valuable insights that stand on their own, Retweeting can help them gain more visibility.

- **Quickly Sharing Something with Your Followers:** If you come across a funny, informative, or trending post and want your audience to see it without extra commentary.

When to Use a Quote Tweet

A **Quote Tweet** is more useful when you want to add **your own perspective, commentary, or context** to a post. Consider using a Quote Tweet in the following situations:

- **Adding Insight:** If someone shares a thought-provoking post, you can Quote Tweet it and add your own analysis or perspective.

- **Starting a Discussion:** You can ask a question or spark a conversation by Quote Tweeting an interesting post.

- **Providing Additional Information:** If a Tweet shares breaking news, you can Quote Tweet it with a link to more details or analysis.

- **Humorous Reactions:** Many users use Quote Tweets to add funny or ironic comments to existing Tweets.

- **Responding Publicly:** If you want to reply to a Tweet but also want your own audience to see it, a Quote Tweet ensures broader visibility.

3. Strategic Ways to Use Retweets and Quote Tweets

Using Retweets and Quote Tweets strategically can **increase your visibility, grow your audience, and improve engagement**. Here are some best practices for both:

Best Practices for Retweets

✅ **Support Other Users:** Retweeting posts from your peers, industry experts, or followers can help build relationships and show appreciation.

✅ **Balance Retweets with Original Content:** If you only Retweet and never post your own content, your feed may seem less engaging.

✅ **Retweet at Peak Times:** If you want your Retweets to reach the maximum audience, share them when your followers are most active.

✅ **Use Retweets to Curate Valuable Content:** If you want to position yourself as a thought leader, Retweeting relevant and insightful content can enhance your credibility.

✅ **Be Selective:** Avoid Retweeting every post you see; focus on content that aligns with your personal or brand values.

Best Practices for Quote Tweets

✅ **Add Value to the Original Post:** Avoid just restating what the Tweet says. Instead, contribute additional insights, questions, or opinions.

✅ **Use Humor and Creativity:** Clever, witty Quote Tweets tend to perform well and encourage engagement.

✅ **Engage in Conversations:** Quote Tweeting can be a great way to interact with influencers and participate in trending discussions.

✅ **Encourage Replies:** Instead of just stating an opinion, ask your audience what they think to drive more engagement.

✅ **Avoid Overusing Quote Tweets:** If you only Quote Tweet and never Retweet or post original content, your profile might feel cluttered with commentary rather than unique thoughts.

4. Common Mistakes to Avoid

While Retweets and Quote Tweets are powerful tools, there are common mistakes users make when using them:

Mistakes with Retweets

❌ **Retweeting Without Verifying Information:** Always check sources before Retweeting news or controversial content.

❌ **Retweeting Too Much at Once:** If you Retweet a lot of posts in a short time, you might flood your followers' feeds and make your profile seem spammy.

❌ **Retweeting Without Adding Context (When Needed):** If a Tweet is vague or lacks necessary background information, consider a Quote Tweet instead.

Mistakes with Quote Tweets

❌ **Using Quote Tweets to Insult or Attack Others:** Engaging in online arguments or negative Quote Tweets can harm your reputation.

❌ **Adding Meaningless Commentary:** Simply writing "Wow" or "This" in a Quote Tweet without context doesn't add value.

❌ **Overusing Quote Tweets Instead of Creating Original Posts:** If all your posts are Quote Tweets, it may appear that you don't have unique content to share.

5. Conclusion

Both Retweets and Quote Tweets are essential engagement tools on X (Twitter). Knowing when and how to use each can help you **build a stronger presence, engage more effectively with your audience, and maximize the reach of your content**.

To summarize:

- Use **Retweets** when you want to **amplify a message without adding personal input**.

- Use **Quote Tweets** when you want to **provide commentary, start discussions, or add value**.

- Always be mindful of **timing, audience, and content quality** when sharing.

By mastering these features, you can make your interactions more impactful and take full advantage of X (Twitter) as a powerful social media platform.

3.2.3 Following and Unfollowing Users

Engaging with others on X (Twitter) is an essential part of building your presence, whether you're using the platform for personal connections, networking, or business purposes. One of the key ways to interact with other users is by **following and unfollowing accounts strategically**. This section will guide you through the **importance of following users, how to follow and unfollow properly, and best practices for managing your follower list effectively**.

1. The Importance of Following Users on X (Twitter)

Following users on X (Twitter) is not just about increasing your follower count—it's about **curating your feed, engaging in meaningful conversations, and expanding your reach**. Here are some key reasons why following the right accounts matters:

Staying Informed and Engaged

- Following industry leaders, news organizations, and experts allows you to stay up to date with trending topics, breaking news, and discussions in your field.

- By following relevant users, you can learn from their insights, share their content, and become part of important conversations.

Building Relationships and Networking

- Following influencers and active users in your niche can help you **establish connections and build your online presence**.

- Engaging with their content by liking, retweeting, and replying can increase the chances of them noticing you and interacting back.

- If you're a business or brand, following your customers, competitors, and partners helps **build engagement and trust**.

Improving Your Feed's Quality

- The more **relevant accounts** you follow, the more valuable content you'll see in your feed.

- Following active and insightful users ensures that your timeline is filled with useful and engaging posts instead of random or low-quality content.

2. How to Follow Users on X (Twitter)

Following someone on X (Twitter) is **simple and can be done in multiple ways**. Below are the different methods you can use to find and follow users.

Following Someone from Their Profile

1. **Search for a user** using the search bar at the top of the app or website.

2. Click on the user's **profile name or handle** to visit their profile page.

3. Click the **Follow** button (a blue button with a plus sign).

4. Once followed, the button will change to **Following**, and their posts will now appear in your timeline.

Tip: Before following someone, check their bio and recent tweets to see if their content aligns with your interests.

Following Someone from Your Timeline

1. If you see a post from someone interesting, tap their **profile picture or name** to open their profile.

2. Click the **Follow** button.

3. You can also tap the **three-dot menu** on the post and select **Follow @username**.

Who to follow

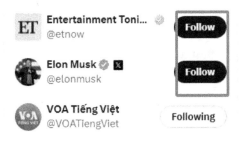

Show more

Following Suggested Users

- X (Twitter) provides **recommendations** based on your interests and activity.

- To find suggested users:

    1. Go to the **"For You" tab** or the "Who to Follow" section.

    2. Browse through the recommended accounts and tap **Follow** on any profile that interests you.

Following Users from a Retweet or Mention

- If someone retweets a post that interests you, click on the **original poster's name** to visit their profile and follow them.

- Similarly, if someone is **mentioned in a tweet** and you find their profile relevant, you can follow them directly.

---

3. How to Unfollow Users on X (Twitter)

Unfollowing users is just as important as following them. Over time, you may find that some accounts no longer provide value, post too frequently, or are no longer relevant to your interests. Here's how to manage your following list effectively.

How to Unfollow Someone

Method 1: From Their Profile

1. Go to the **user's profile page**.

2. Click on the **Following** button (which indicates you are following them).

3. The button will change to **Unfollow**—click it again to confirm.

Show more

Method 2: From Your Following List

1. Navigate to your profile and click on **Following** to see the list of users you follow.

2. Find the user you want to unfollow and click the **Following** button next to their name.

3. Select **Unfollow** to remove them.

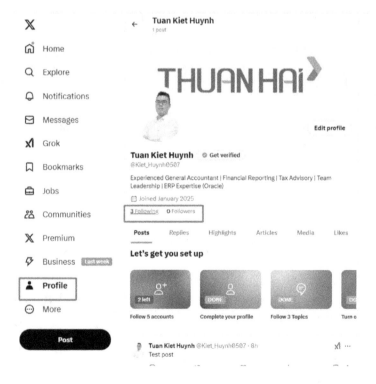

Method 3: From Your Timeline

1. If you see a tweet from someone you no longer want to follow, tap the **three-dot menu** on their post.

2. Select **Unfollow @username**.

Method 4: Using X (Twitter) Lists

- If you don't want to completely unfollow someone but still want to limit their visibility in your feed, you can:

    o **Mute them** (so their tweets don't appear in your feed).

    o **Add them to a private list** so you can check their updates when you want.

---

4. Best Practices for Following and Unfollowing Users

Be Selective About Who You Follow

- Avoid **follow-for-follow** strategies that result in a cluttered feed.

- Follow users who provide **valuable content** relevant to your interests or industry.

Engage Before Unfollowing

- If you're considering unfollowing someone due to inactivity, first check if they are still relevant.

- Try engaging with their latest content before deciding to remove them.

Regularly Clean Up Your Following List

- Periodically **review who you follow** and remove accounts that:

    o Post **too frequently** or spam content.

    o Are **inactive** for months.

    o No longer align with your interests.

Avoid Mass Following and Unfollowing

- Rapidly following or unfollowing users in bulk can **trigger X's (Twitter's) spam detection**, potentially leading to account suspension.

- Instead, follow and unfollow users **gradually** over time.

Use Third-Party Tools for Management

- If you follow a large number of accounts, you can use tools like:

  - **TweetDeck** (for better organization).

  - **CircleBoom** or **ManageFlitter** (to analyze inactive followers and unfollow non-engaging accounts).

5. Final Thoughts

Following and unfollowing users on X (Twitter) is **more than just a numbers game**—it's about creating a high-quality feed, engaging with meaningful content, and expanding your reach strategically. By following the right people, regularly curating your following list, and interacting with your audience, you can **build a strong, relevant, and engaging presence on X**.

Next, we'll dive deeper into **"Understanding the Algorithm"**, where we explore **how X (Twitter) ranks content, factors that boost engagement, and why some tweets go viral**.

Summary of Key Takeaways:

✓ Follow **relevant** users to build an engaging and informative feed.
✓ Use multiple methods to find and follow users, including **profile search, timeline suggestions, and mentions**.
✓ Unfollow users who are **inactive, irrelevant, or spammy**, but do so gradually.
✓ Regularly clean up your following list to ensure **high-quality engagement**.
✓ Avoid **mass-following and unfollowing**, as this can lead to restrictions.
✓ Use **third-party tools** to manage and analyze your following strategy.

3.3 Understanding the Algorithm

3.3.1 How X (Twitter) Ranks Content

Introduction

Understanding how X (formerly Twitter) ranks content is essential for maximizing engagement and visibility on the platform. Unlike chronological feeds of the past, X uses a complex algorithm to determine which posts appear on users' timelines. This ranking system prioritizes content based on relevance, engagement, and user preferences rather than simply displaying tweets in real-time order.

This section will explore how the X ranking algorithm works, the key factors influencing tweet visibility, and actionable strategies to optimize content for better reach.

How the X (Twitter) Algorithm Works

X employs machine learning and artificial intelligence to personalize each user's experience. The algorithm analyzes numerous data points to predict which tweets a user is most likely to find interesting.

There are three primary timeline views that influence how content is ranked:

1. **For You Feed:** A mix of recommended tweets from accounts you follow and those you don't, curated based on your activity and engagement history.

2. **Following Feed:** Tweets displayed in reverse chronological order from accounts you follow, with no algorithmic ranking.

3. **Trending and Explore Sections:** Content is ranked based on trending topics, popular hashtags, and user interests.

When a tweet is published, the algorithm evaluates its potential reach based on initial engagement. The more interactions (likes, retweets, replies) a tweet gets in its early stages, the more likely it is to be amplified to a larger audience.

Key Factors That Influence X (Twitter) Content Ranking

1. User Engagement Signals

Engagement is the most critical factor in ranking content on X. The algorithm prioritizes tweets that generate significant interactions, including:

- **Likes:** Indicate approval and increase a tweet's visibility.

- **Retweets & Quote Tweets:** Amplify content to a wider audience.

- **Replies & Conversations:** Encourage discussion and improve ranking.

- **Shares via Direct Messages (DMs):** Suggest strong user interest.

Tweets with higher engagement rates are shown more frequently on the **For You** feed. The algorithm also favors conversations where multiple users interact with a post, keeping discussions alive for longer periods.

2. Recency and Freshness

While engagement is crucial, recency also plays a role in content ranking. The algorithm gives preference to newer tweets, particularly in the **Following** feed. However, older tweets can still gain traction if they continue to receive interactions over time.

- **New tweets with fast-growing engagement are pushed to the For You feed.**

- **Evergreen content can resurface if it remains relevant.**

- **Time zones and active hours impact visibility (tweets posted during peak hours have higher chances of engagement).**

3. Personalization and User Behavior

Each user's feed is customized based on their past activity. The algorithm takes into account:

- **Accounts frequently engaged with (liked, retweeted, or replied to).**

- **Topics of interest (based on interactions and search behavior).**

- **Tweets from users similar to those they already follow.**

If a user regularly engages with tweets about **technology**, for example, the algorithm will prioritize tweets from tech influencers or topics related to that niche.

4. Relevance to Current Trends and Events

Trending topics and breaking news have a higher chance of appearing in users' feeds. The algorithm detects:

- **Hashtags and keywords related to viral discussions.**

- **Posts that contribute to trending conversations.**

- **Tweets from verified accounts or influential figures covering real-time events.**

For example, during major sports events or political debates, tweets using related hashtags gain more visibility.

5. Multimedia Content (Images, Videos, and GIFs)

The algorithm favors visual content over plain text tweets. Posts that include **videos, high-quality images, and GIFs** tend to generate more engagement, leading to:

- **Higher interaction rates compared to text-only tweets.**

- **Better ranking in the For You feed.**

- **Increased shares and discussions.**

Native videos (directly uploaded to X) perform better than external links (such as YouTube links). The algorithm prioritizes content that keeps users on the platform.

6. Link Sharing and External Content

While X allows external links, tweets with outbound links may receive lower organic reach. The platform prefers to keep users engaged within its ecosystem. To counteract this:

- **Use compelling captions to encourage clicks.**

- **Mix link-based tweets with native content.**

- **Engage with followers before and after sharing links.**

However, verified accounts and media organizations often have higher link engagement due to credibility.

7. Verified Accounts and Twitter Blue

X gives priority to tweets from **verified accounts and Twitter Blue subscribers**, as they are considered more credible. Benefits include:

- **Increased visibility in replies and searches.**

- **Higher ranking in algorithm-driven feeds.**

- **Access to premium engagement features (such as extended tweets and priority notifications).**

Strategies to Optimize Content for Higher Ranking

To increase tweet visibility and engagement, consider these best practices:

1. Craft Engaging and Interactive Tweets

- Ask questions or encourage discussions to boost replies.
- Use call-to-action phrases (e.g., "Retweet if you agree!").
- Keep tweets concise and easy to read (ideal length: 70-100 characters).

2. Post at Peak Engagement Times

- Best times: **Morning (8–10 AM) and Evening (6–9 PM)**
- Avoid low-traffic hours (late nights or early mornings).
- Analyze audience activity using **X Analytics**.

3. Leverage Hashtags and Trends

- Use **1-3 relevant hashtags** per tweet.
- Monitor trending topics and join relevant conversations.
- Create branded hashtags for campaigns.

4. Engage with Other Users

- Reply to trending tweets to gain exposure.
- Retweet industry leaders to increase visibility.
- Participate in Spaces and live discussions.

5. Use High-Quality Media

- Post **high-resolution images and engaging videos**.
- Create **short-form video content (5-30 seconds)**.
- Optimize captions for clarity and impact.

6. Maintain Consistency

- Tweet **regularly (3-5 times per day)** to stay active.
- Schedule posts using **Twitter's scheduling tools**.
- Maintain a consistent brand voice.

7. Monitor Analytics and Adjust Strategy

- Use **X Analytics** to track engagement.
- Identify high-performing tweets and replicate success.
- Adjust content strategy based on audience insights.

Conclusion

X's ranking algorithm is designed to surface engaging, relevant, and high-quality content. By understanding how tweets are ranked, users can optimize their content strategy to maximize visibility and engagement.

The key takeaways include:

- **Engagement drives visibility**—focus on likes, replies, and retweets.
- **Recency matters**, but evergreen content can still perform well.
- **Personalization affects ranking**—build relationships with your audience.
- **Trends, multimedia, and verified accounts gain higher exposure.**

Mastering these principles will help users grow their presence on X and create impactful content that reaches a wider audience.

3.3.2 Factors That Boost Engagement

Engagement on X (Twitter) is a key metric that determines how well your content is received by your audience. High engagement means more likes, retweets, comments, and shares, which can help expand your reach and influence. To maximize engagement, it is essential to understand the factors that influence how people interact with your posts and how the X (Twitter) algorithm prioritizes content.

In this section, we will explore the key factors that boost engagement and provide actionable strategies to help you optimize your posts for better visibility and interaction.

1. Posting High-Quality and Relevant Content

Content is the foundation of engagement on X (Twitter). To attract and retain audience interaction, your tweets should be:

- **Relevant:** Your content should align with the interests of your target audience. Stay updated with trending topics in your niche.

- **Valuable:** Provide information, entertainment, or inspiration that makes people want to engage.

- **Clear and Concise:** Since X (Twitter) has a character limit, your message should be impactful and easy to read.

- **Engaging:** Use questions, polls, and open-ended statements to encourage replies.

Best Practices:

✅ Stay updated with trending topics and join relevant conversations.

✅ Use storytelling techniques to make your tweets more engaging.

✅ Share useful insights, tips, or personal experiences to add value.

2. Timing Your Tweets for Maximum Engagement

Posting at the right time significantly impacts engagement. If you post when your audience is most active, you increase the chances of getting immediate interaction, which helps the algorithm prioritize your content.

How to Find the Best Posting Time

- **Analyze Your Audience:** Use X (Twitter) Analytics or third-party tools like Buffer and Hootsuite to track when your followers are online.

- **Experiment with Different Times:** Try posting in the morning, afternoon, and evening to see when you get the most engagement.

- **Follow General Best Practices:** Studies suggest that the best times to post are:

    o **Weekdays:** 9 AM – 11 AM (morning engagement) and 6 PM – 9 PM (evening engagement)

    o **Weekends:** Engagement tends to be lower, but Sunday evenings can be effective.

Best Practices:

✓ Post when your target audience is most active.

✓ Experiment with different time slots and analyze performance.

✓ Schedule tweets in advance using scheduling tools to maintain consistency.

---

3. Using Visuals to Increase Engagement

Tweets with images, GIFs, and videos tend to get higher engagement than text-only posts. Visuals make your content stand out in a fast-moving feed.

Types of Visual Content That Perform Well

- **High-Quality Images:** Use eye-catching graphics or infographics to make complex information easier to digest.

- **Videos:** Short-form videos (under 1 minute) tend to perform well, especially if they are informative or entertaining.

- **GIFs:** A fun way to add personality and humor to your tweets.

- **Memes:** If used appropriately, memes can boost relatability and shareability.

Best Practices:

✓ Use visuals that are relevant to your message.

✓ Ensure images and videos are high-resolution and properly formatted.

✓ Add captions or text overlays to make content more accessible.

---

4. Writing Engaging Captions and Calls to Action (CTA)

Your tweet's text should encourage interaction. Adding a **call to action (CTA)** can prompt users to like, reply, or retweet.

Examples of Effective CTAs:

- **For Engagement:** "What do you think? Reply below!"

- **For Retweets:** "If you agree, retweet this!"

- **For Clicks:** "Check out this article for more details [link]."

- **For Polls:** "Vote now! Which one do you prefer?"

Best Practices:

✓ Keep captions concise but impactful.

✓ Use a friendly, conversational tone.

✓ Ask open-ended questions to spark discussions.

---

5. Leveraging Hashtags for Discoverability

Hashtags help categorize your tweets and increase their reach beyond your followers. Using the right hashtags can expose your content to a larger audience.

How to Use Hashtags Effectively

- **Use Relevant Hashtags:** Stick to hashtags related to your content and audience.

- **Limit the Number of Hashtags:** 1-3 hashtags per tweet is ideal for engagement.

- **Join Trending Conversations:** Engaging with trending hashtags can help you reach more users.

- **Create Branded Hashtags:** If you have a personal brand or business, consider creating a unique hashtag.

Best Practices:

✓ Research popular hashtags in your niche using tools like Hashtagify.

✓ Combine broad and niche-specific hashtags.

✓ Monitor hashtag performance to refine your strategy.

---

6. Engaging with Other Users and Communities

Engagement is a two-way street. The more you interact with others, the more likely they are to engage with you.

Ways to Engage Actively

- **Reply to Comments:** Show appreciation for replies and keep the conversation going.

- **Retweet and Quote Tweet Others:** Sharing valuable content from others encourages reciprocal engagement.

- **Participate in Twitter Chats and Spaces:** Joining discussions in your industry helps build your presence.

Best Practices:
✓ Be genuine and authentic in your interactions.
✓ Reply to comments quickly to keep the conversation active.
✓ Engage with industry leaders and influencers to expand your reach.

---

7. Posting Consistently to Stay Visible

Consistency is key to maintaining audience engagement and visibility. The more frequently you post, the higher the chances of staying in users' feeds.

How to Maintain Consistency

- **Create a Posting Schedule:** Plan your tweets in advance to maintain regular activity.

- **Use Scheduling Tools:** Platforms like Buffer, Hootsuite, and TweetDeck help automate posting.

- **Maintain a Content Mix:** Balance between informational, entertaining, and promotional tweets.

Best Practices:
✓ Post at least 3-5 times per day for steady engagement.
✓ Maintain a balance between real-time engagement and scheduled posts.
✓ Analyze what types of content perform best and refine your strategy.

---

8. Encouraging Engagement with Polls and Interactive Features

Polls, threads, and interactive tweets can drive higher engagement by inviting user participation.

How to Use Polls Effectively

- **Ask Simple and Relevant Questions:** Polls should be easy to answer.

- **Keep Options Limited:** 2-4 choices work best.

- **Follow Up with Engagement:** Discuss poll results in a thread.

Best Practices:

✅ Run polls regularly to boost engagement.

✅ Use polls for market research or audience feedback.

✅ Follow up with discussions on poll results.

Final Thoughts

Boosting engagement on X (Twitter) requires a combination of high-quality content, strategic posting, active interaction, and leveraging platform features. By consistently applying these best practices, you can build a strong presence and maximize audience engagement.

3.3.3 Why Some Tweets Go Viral

Going viral on X (Twitter) is the ultimate goal for many users, whether they are individuals looking to grow their personal brand, businesses seeking more exposure, or content creators aiming for greater engagement. However, virality is not just about luck—it is a combination of strategic content creation, understanding the platform's algorithm, and leveraging human psychology. In this section, we will explore why some tweets go viral, the key elements that contribute to virality, and actionable strategies to increase your chances of creating viral content.

The Science Behind Virality

Virality on X (Twitter) happens when a post gains a rapid increase in engagement (likes, retweets, replies, and shares), causing it to spread exponentially beyond the creator's immediate audience. The platform's algorithm prioritizes content with high engagement, pushing it to more users through recommendations, trending topics, and explore feeds.

A viral tweet typically has the following characteristics:

1. **Emotional Appeal** – Tweets that evoke strong emotions such as happiness, surprise, anger, or nostalgia are more likely to be shared.

2. **Relatability** – Content that resonates with a large audience, making people say, "That's so true!" encourages engagement.

3. **Novelty and Originality** – Unique insights, fresh perspectives, or creative humor stand out.

4. **Brevity and Clarity** – Short, impactful tweets perform better than long-winded ones.

5. **Engagement Loops** – Encouraging participation through questions, polls, or call-to-actions (CTAs) leads to more interactions.

6. **Trend Utilization** – Leveraging trending hashtags, news, or viral challenges increases visibility.

Let's break down these elements in detail and learn how to apply them effectively.

1. Emotional Triggers: The Heart of Virality

Human psychology plays a huge role in what gets shared on social media. Tweets that spark strong emotions are significantly more likely to be engaged with and spread across the platform.

The Most Viral Emotions

According to studies on social media virality, the most shareable emotions include:

- **Happiness & Humor** – Funny tweets, memes, and witty commentary often get shared the most.

- **Surprise & Curiosity** – Unexpected facts, shocking revelations, or intriguing questions attract attention.

- **Anger & Controversy** – While risky, polarizing tweets that spark debates often gain traction.

- **Inspiration & Motivation** – Uplifting stories, quotes, and success tips encourage retweets.

How to Apply Emotional Triggers

- Use humor: Craft witty one-liners, sarcastic observations, or relatable jokes.

- Share inspiring stories: Personal achievements, motivational experiences, or positive news tend to perform well.

- Ask thought-provoking questions: Challenge perspectives and encourage discussions.

Example of a viral emotional tweet:

"I started my business with just $10 and a dream. Today, I employ 50 people. Never let anyone tell you it's impossible."

---

2. Relatability: Making People Feel Seen

Relatable content makes people feel connected, leading them to share it with others.

What Makes a Tweet Relatable?

- Shared struggles and experiences (e.g., work stress, relationships, daily life).

- Popular culture references that resonate with a broad audience.

- Common frustrations or challenges people face.

How to Craft Relatable Content

- Use "We all know that feeling when…" style posts.

- Tap into universal experiences, like running out of phone battery or waking up late.

- Exaggerate common scenarios for comedic effect.

Example of a viral relatable tweet:

"Me: I'll sleep early tonight.
Also me at 3 AM: Let's watch one more episode."

3. The Power of Novelty and Originality

In a sea of repetitive content, tweets that present unique insights, fresh takes, or original humor stand out.

How to Be Original on X (Twitter)

- Offer a new perspective on a trending topic.

- Share rare knowledge or little-known facts.

- Create a unique challenge, hashtag, or meme.

Examples of Viral Original Tweets

- *"Here's a productivity hack that changed my life: Write tomorrow's to-do list before you sleep. Your brain starts working on it overnight."*

- *"Why does no one talk about how the first 10 minutes of any Zoom call is just 'Can you hear me?' 'You're muted!' 'Try rejoining!'"*

4. Clarity and Brevity: The Art of Concise Tweets

X (Twitter) has a character limit, meaning concise, to-the-point tweets are more effective than long ones.

The Formula for a Perfect Short Tweet

- **Keep it under 150 characters.**

- **Use simple words and direct language.**

- **Use line breaks to improve readability.**

Example of a Short Viral Tweet

"Success = Consistency + Patience + Learning from Failures."

5. Engagement Loops: Encouraging Interaction

Tweets that invite engagement get amplified by the algorithm.

How to Boost Engagement

- **Ask Questions:** "What's the best career advice you've ever received?"

- **Use Polls:** "Which social media platform do you use the most? [ ] X (Twitter) [ ] Instagram [ ] TikTok [ ] LinkedIn"

- **Encourage Retweets:** "Retweet if you've ever experienced this!"

Example of a viral engagement tweet:

"What's a piece of advice that changed your life? I'll go first: 'Done is better than perfect.'"

---

6. Leveraging Trends: Riding the Wave of Popularity

X (Twitter) has a dynamic trending system, and tweets that align with trending topics often gain more exposure.

How to Use Trends to Go Viral

- Monitor the "Trending" and "For You" sections.

- Jump on viral memes or cultural moments.

- Use trending hashtags effectively.

Example of a Viral Trend-Based Tweet

If a celebrity gives an iconic speech, you can tweet:
"If [celebrity name] can do THAT, I can definitely finish my to-do list today!"

Conclusion: Crafting Your Own Viral Tweet Strategy

While there is no guaranteed formula for virality, understanding these key principles can significantly increase your chances:

✓ Evoke strong emotions
✓ Make content relatable
✓ Be unique and original
✓ Keep tweets concise and impactful
✓ Encourage engagement through questions and CTAs
✓ Tap into trending topics

Now that you understand what makes tweets go viral, start experimenting with different styles and see what resonates with your audience. Who knows? Your next tweet might just be the one that takes off!

1. Emotional Appeal: Humor and Relatability

Example: *"Me trying to eat healthy: [picture of a salad]*
Also me after seeing pizza: [picture of a pizza slice]"
This tweet went viral because it combined humor and relatability, tapping into a common experience of struggling to eat healthily.

Why it worked:

- **Humor**: The tweet was funny, which makes it more likely to be shared.

- **Relatability**: Many people struggle with making healthy choices, especially when it comes to food, making it highly relatable.

2. Surprise and Curiosity

Example: *"I just found out that octopuses have three hearts. If you're still wondering if 2020 can get weirder, it can."*
This tweet gained viral attention because it shared an unexpected and intriguing fact that sparked curiosity.

Why it worked:

- **Surprise**: The fun, strange fact caught people's attention.

- **Curiosity**: The mention of "2020" added a touch of humor, making readers curious about the oddity.

3. Trend Utilization: Riding the Popular Wave

Example: During the "Game of Thrones" series finale, many people tweeted about their disappointment with how the show ended, using the hashtag #NotMyJonSnow. This tweet from a popular Twitter user stood out:

"I've never been more disappointed in my life, and I watched The Red Wedding live." This tweet capitalized on the "Game of Thrones" fandom and the ongoing conversation about the controversial ending.

Why it worked:

- **Timeliness**: The tweet was part of a larger trending conversation, which helped it gain attention.

- **Relatability**: The tweet humorously references a previous shocking event in the show, resonating with other fans.

---

4. Engagement Loop: Asking a Question

Example: *"What's the worst advice you've ever received? I'll go first: 'Just follow your passion.'"*

This tweet generated tons of replies from people sharing their worst advice, creating an engagement loop where the user prompted others to share their own stories.

Why it worked:

- **Encouraging Replies**: By asking a question, the tweet encouraged followers to engage and share their own experiences.

- **Relatability**: Many people have received bad advice, making the content resonate with a broad audience.

---

5. Originality: Unique Take on a Trend

Example: In response to the #ThrowbackThursday trend, a creative user posted a tweet with an old childhood photo and captioned it:
"Me before I knew the struggles of adulthood. #TBT"
This tweet went viral because it added a unique perspective on a popular trend.

Why it worked:

- **Creativity**: The user put a fresh spin on the usual #TBT posts.

- **Relatability**: Many people feel nostalgic about their childhood and the ease of life before adulthood's responsibilities.

6. Controversial Content: Sparking Debate

Example: *"I honestly don't get why people love pineapple on pizza. Fight me."* This tweet quickly garnered retweets and replies, sparking a heated debate over the controversial topic of pineapple on pizza.

Why it worked:

- **Polarization**: It created a divide, with people either agreeing or disagreeing, generating a lot of engagement.

- **Engagement**: The invitation to "fight me" in a playful tone encouraged people to respond and debate.

7. Inspirational Content: Motivational Tweet

Example: *"The best way to predict the future is to create it."* This simple motivational quote from Abraham Lincoln was shared widely, inspiring many to share their own experiences or thoughts on success.

Why it worked:

- **Inspiration**: Motivational content often resonates deeply with people, inspiring them to share it.

- **Clarity**: The tweet was short, impactful, and easy to understand, making it highly shareable.

CHAPTER III
Advanced Features on X (Twitter)

4.1 Using Threads for Long-Form Content

4.1.1 How to Create an Engaging Thread

Introduction to Threads

X (formerly Twitter) is known for its concise and fast-paced nature, but sometimes, a single post (tweet) isn't enough to share in-depth thoughts, insights, or stories. This is where **Threads** come in. A thread is a series of connected posts that allow you to present a more detailed narrative, break down complex ideas, or guide your audience through step-by-step instructions.

Creating an engaging thread requires a combination of structure, clarity, and engagement techniques. In this section, we'll explore how to craft an effective thread that captivates your audience, encourages interactions, and maximizes visibility.

1. Planning Your Thread Content

Before you start writing a thread, it's important to plan your content. Unlike a single tweet, which should be concise and to the point, a thread needs a clear **flow** and **structure**. Here are key steps to consider when planning your thread:

Define Your Goal

Ask yourself: **What is the purpose of this thread?** Common thread objectives include:

- **Explaining a complex concept** (e.g., "How AI is revolutionizing marketing")

- **Telling a compelling story** (e.g., "How I grew my startup from zero to $100K in revenue")

- **Sharing insights or lessons learned** (e.g., "5 mistakes I made as a beginner investor")

- **Providing a tutorial or step-by-step guide** (e.g., "How to run a successful ad campaign on X")

Having a clear objective will help you keep the thread focused and valuable to your audience.

Organize Your Main Points

Break down your topic into **logical sections** or **key points**. Each tweet in the thread should contribute to the overall story or argument. A good structure to follow is:

- **Introduction (Hook)**: Grabs attention and sets expectations.

- **Key Points (Body)**: Each tweet adds value, building upon the previous one.

- **Conclusion (Call to Action or Summary)**: Reinforces the message and encourages engagement.

2. Writing an Effective Hook (First Tweet)

Your **first tweet** is the most important part of your thread. This is where you need to **capture attention** and **encourage users to read further**. Here are some techniques to craft a powerful hook:

Start with a Bold Statement

Make a strong, thought-provoking statement that piques curiosity.

- **Example**: *"Most people fail at social media marketing because they ignore this one simple strategy. Let's break it down in this thread. 📌👇"*

Ask a Thought-Provoking Question

Encouraging curiosity through a question can make readers want to find out the answer.

- **Example**: *"Have you ever wondered why some people gain thousands of followers in a few months while others struggle? Here's the secret. 👇"*

Use a Teaser

Make a promise about what readers will gain by reading the thread.

- **Example**: *"I just made $10,000 in 30 days using a simple email marketing technique. Here's the full breakdown (step by step). 📋👇"*

Use Numbers or Lists

Numbers help structure expectations and make your content more digestible.

- **Example**: *"7 powerful productivity hacks that will help you get more done in less time. Let's dive in. 👇"*

---

3. Writing the Body of Your Thread

Once you have a compelling hook, the next step is crafting the **body** of your thread. Each tweet should contribute to the main topic while keeping the reader engaged.

Make Each Tweet Valuable

Every tweet should stand alone with **useful, interesting, or insightful** content. Avoid filler text or unnecessary details.

- **Good Example**:
  - *Tweet 1: "1. Start your day by writing down your top 3 priorities. This forces you to focus on what truly matters."*
  - *Tweet 2: "2. Use the Pomodoro technique: Work for 25 minutes, then take a 5-minute break. This boosts productivity and prevents burnout."*

- **Bad Example**:
  - *Tweet 1: "Let's talk about productivity."*
  - *Tweet 2: "It's important to stay focused."*

Use Formatting for Readability

People skim through X (Twitter) content quickly, so make your thread easy to digest.

- **Use short sentences** and **line breaks** to avoid walls of text.

- **Use emojis** sparingly to highlight key points (e.g., ✓, ✗, 💡).
- **Use numbers or bullet points** to structure information.

Keep the Momentum Going

Each tweet should flow naturally into the next. One technique is using **cliffhangers** to keep the reader engaged.

- **Example**: *"That's not all. The next tip will completely change the way you manage your time. Keep reading. 👇"*

4. Ending Your Thread Effectively

Your last tweet should **wrap up the thread** and encourage engagement. Here's how to do it effectively:

Summarize Key Takeaways

Reinforce the main points of your thread.

- **Example**: *"To summarize: (1) Prioritize your tasks, (2) Use the Pomodoro technique, (3) Limit distractions, and (4) Take strategic breaks. Follow these, and you'll see a huge boost in productivity!"*

Call to Action (CTA)

Encourage readers to interact by:

- Asking a question: *"Which of these strategies have you tried? Let me know in the comments! 👇"*
- Inviting retweets: *"If you found this helpful, share it with others! 🔁"*
- Directing them to more content: *"Follow me for more marketing tips every week! 🚀"*

5. Optimizing Your Thread for Maximum Reach

To ensure your thread reaches a **wider audience**, follow these best practices:

Post at the Right Time

- Identify when your audience is **most active** (usually mornings and evenings).

- Use X (Twitter) analytics to find your **optimal posting time**.

Engage with Comments

- Reply to people who comment on your thread.

- Ask follow-up questions to keep the conversation going.

Pin Your Best Threads

- If your thread is valuable, **pin it** to your profile for new visitors to see.

6. How to Post a Thread on X (Twitter)

Posting a thread on X (Twitter) is simple, but to do it effectively, you need to follow a structured process. Below is a step-by-step guide to creating and posting a thread.

Step 1: Start Your First Tweet (The Hook)

1. **Open X (Twitter)** on your desktop or mobile app.

2. **Click on the "Post" button** (formerly "Tweet" button).

3. Type your **first tweet**, which should be your **hook** (a compelling statement, question, or teaser).

4. Before posting, make sure this first tweet **grabs attention** and gives users a reason to read the rest.

5. **Don't hit "Post" yet!** Instead, proceed to Step 2.

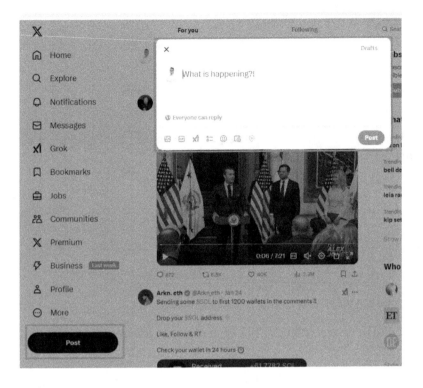

Step 2: Add More Tweets to Create a Thread

1. Below your first tweet, click **the "+" button** (on mobile) or **"Add another post"** (on desktop).

2. A new tweet box will appear where you can continue your thread.

3. Keep adding tweets by clicking the **"+" button** until your thread is complete.

Tip: Each tweet should be **concise** but informative. Aim for **one key idea per tweet**.

Step 3: Review Your Thread Before Posting

1. Read through your entire thread to **check for clarity, typos, and flow**.

2. Make sure the **tweets are logically connected** and keep the reader engaged.

3. **Use line breaks, bullet points, and emojis** to improve readability.

4. If needed, rearrange or edit tweets before posting.

Step 4: Post the Thread

1. Once satisfied, click **"Post all"** (or "Tweet all" on some versions).

2. X (Twitter) will publish your entire thread **in sequence**, making each tweet a reply to the previous one.

Step 5: Engage with Your Audience

1. **Pin your thread** (click the three dots on the first tweet → select "Pin to Profile").

2. **Reply to comments** to encourage discussions and increase engagement.

3. **Retweet or quote tweet** your thread later to keep it visible.

4. Share your thread on other platforms (LinkedIn, Instagram Stories, etc.) to attract more readers.

Bonus: Scheduling a Thread (Optional)

- You can use third-party tools like **Typefully, ThreadStart, Hypefury, or Buffer** to **schedule** your threads in advance.

- This is helpful if you want to post at the **best time for engagement** without manually doing it.

🔥 **That's it! You've successfully posted a thread on X (Twitter).** Now, track its performance using **Twitter Analytics**, and keep improving your strategy!

Conclusion

Creating an engaging thread on X (Twitter) is a powerful way to share detailed content, grow your audience, and establish authority in your niche. By crafting a compelling hook, structuring your content effectively, and encouraging engagement, you can maximize your reach and impact.

4.1.2 Best Practices for Thread Engagement

Twitter threads are a powerful tool for delivering long-form content in a structured and engaging way. However, simply posting a series of connected tweets isn't enough to ensure engagement. To maximize the impact of your threads, you need to craft them strategically, keeping your audience engaged from the first tweet to the last. This section explores best practices to help you create compelling and interactive threads that boost your visibility, encourage interactions, and enhance your Twitter presence.

1. Start with a Strong Hook

The first tweet in your thread is the most critical because it determines whether users will click "Show this thread" and continue reading. A weak opening can result in people scrolling past without engaging.

How to Write a Strong Hook:

- **Ask a thought-provoking question**: "What if I told you that one Twitter thread could change your entire social media strategy?"

- **Make a bold statement**: "Most people are using Twitter threads the WRONG way. Here's how to fix it."

- **Tease the value of the thread**: "I grew my Twitter audience by 10,000 followers in 6 months using this simple Twitter thread formula. Let me break it down."

By crafting a compelling hook, you immediately capture your audience's attention and entice them to read further.

2. Structure Your Thread for Readability

People tend to skim through content on social media, so your thread should be structured for easy reading.

Key Formatting Tips:

- **Use short sentences and paragraphs**: Long, dense tweets can overwhelm readers. Keep each tweet concise.

- **Number your points**: If your thread contains a step-by-step guide, numbering each step (e.g., "Step 1: Choose a strong hook") makes it easier to follow.

- **Use spacing and line breaks**: This enhances readability, making tweets less intimidating.

- **Utilize bold words or emojis**: This helps highlight key points (e.g., "🔥 Pro tip: Start your thread with a compelling question.").

3. Provide Value in Every Tweet

Each tweet in your thread should offer value, whether through insights, actionable advice, or entertainment. Avoid filler content that doesn't contribute meaningfully to the thread's topic.

How to Ensure Value in Every Tweet:

- **Include useful examples**: Instead of saying "Engagement is important," show why: "Engagement increases your visibility. Here's an example: When I replied to a trending tweet, my impressions skyrocketed by 500%."

- **Use data and facts**: Back up your claims with numbers: "Studies show that tweets with questions generate 21% more engagement."

- **Share personal experiences**: People love relatable content. A real-life story makes your thread more engaging and credible.

4. End Each Tweet with a Micro-CTA

A "micro-CTA" (Call to Action) at the end of each tweet nudges readers to continue engaging with your thread.

Examples of Micro-CTAs:

- "What do you think so far? Let me know in the comments below! 👇"

- "Keep reading... it gets better! ↓🔥"

- "Next up: The biggest mistake people make when writing threads."

Micro-CTAs help maintain engagement throughout the thread and encourage users to interact with your content.

---

5. Use Multimedia to Enhance Engagement

Twitter allows images, GIFs, and videos in tweets. Incorporating these elements makes your thread more visually appealing and engaging.

How to Use Multimedia Effectively:

- **Use relevant images**: If your thread is about social media growth, show screenshots of analytics.

- **Add GIFs or memes**: These add personality and make your thread more fun.

- **Embed charts or infographics**: These help visualize complex data.

- **Include a short video**: A quick 30-second explainer can make your thread stand out.

---

6. Encourage Engagement by Asking Questions

Threads that invite interaction perform better because Twitter's algorithm favors content that sparks discussions.

How to Encourage Responses:

- "Have you tried this strategy before? Drop your thoughts below! 👇"

- "What's the best Twitter thread you've read recently? Share the link in the comments!"

- "Do you agree with this approach, or do you have a different method? Let's discuss."

By directly prompting readers to reply, you boost engagement and make your content more visible on the platform.

7. End with a Strong Call to Action (CTA)

Your final tweet should leave readers with a clear action to take, whether it's following you, subscribing to a newsletter, or sharing the thread.

Effective CTAs for Threads:

- **Encourage sharing**: "If this thread helped you, give it a retweet so more people can benefit! □"

- **Invite them to follow you**: "I share Twitter growth tips like this every week. Follow me for more insights! 🚀"

- **Promote additional content**: "Want more social media strategies? Subscribe to my newsletter for exclusive tips!"

A strong CTA ensures that your thread doesn't just inform but also helps you grow your audience.

8. Monitor and Respond to Engagement

Once your thread is live, your job isn't over! Actively engaging with comments increases its reach and fosters a stronger community.

Best Practices for Managing Engagement:

- **Reply to comments promptly**: Engaging with early responders encourages more people to join the conversation.

- **Quote-tweet interesting replies**: This highlights discussions and keeps the thread active.

- **Pin the thread to your profile**: This increases visibility for new visitors to your profile.

9. Experiment and Analyze Performance

Not every thread will perform equally well. Analyzing your results helps refine your strategy for future threads.

How to Track Performance:

- Use **Twitter Analytics** to check engagement metrics (likes, retweets, impressions).

- Identify **which tweets had the most engagement** and adjust your future hooks accordingly.

- Experiment with **posting times** to see when your audience is most active.

Testing different formats and styles will help you discover what resonates best with your followers.

Final Thoughts

Creating engaging Twitter threads is a skill that improves with practice. By crafting strong hooks, structuring content effectively, providing value, using multimedia, and encouraging interaction, you can maximize engagement and build a stronger presence on Twitter.

4.2 Spaces: Live Audio Conversations

4.2.1 How to Host and Join Spaces

Introduction to Spaces

Spaces is X (formerly Twitter)'s live audio feature that allows users to host real-time conversations with their audience. Similar to Clubhouse and other social audio platforms, Spaces provides an opportunity for users to engage in discussions, share insights, and connect with a broader community in an interactive format. Unlike tweets, which are static, Spaces enable dynamic conversations where multiple participants can talk, listen, and engage in real-time.

Hosting or joining a Space is relatively simple, but to make the most out of it, users should understand the technical aspects, engagement strategies, and best practices for effective moderation. This section will guide you through the process of hosting and joining Spaces, along with tips for maximizing audience participation and conversation quality.

1. Understanding Spaces: The Basics

Before diving into the technical details, it's essential to understand how Spaces work and why they are beneficial.

Key Features of Spaces

- **Live Audio Conversations** – Unlike traditional tweets, Spaces allow users to speak and engage in real-time discussions.

- **Public Accessibility** – Anyone on X can join a Space unless it is restricted by the host.

- **Multiple Speakers** – A Space can have up to 10 speakers simultaneously, including the host.

- **Live Captions** – Automatic captions make Spaces accessible to users with hearing impairments.

- **Replays and Recording** – Hosts can record Spaces and share them for later listening.

- **Audience Engagement** – Listeners can react with emojis, request to speak, and share the Space with their followers.

Benefits of Hosting a Space

- **Build Community** – Spaces allow you to engage with your audience in a more personal and interactive way.

- **Share Expertise** – You can use Spaces to position yourself as an expert in your field.

- **Expand Your Reach** – Live conversations are more likely to be promoted in users' timelines, helping you gain visibility.

- **Real-Time Feedback** – Unlike tweets, which require users to reply or quote, Spaces allow instant discussions and engagement.

2. How to Host a Space on X

If you want to start a live audio conversation, follow these steps to create and manage your own Space.

Creating a Space

1. **Open the X App**

    o   Spaces are currently only available on the X mobile app (iOS and Android).

    o   Ensure your app is updated to access the latest features.

2. **Tap the "+" Button**

    o   On the bottom navigation bar, tap the "+" button (Compose Tweet).

    o   Select **"Start a Space"** from the options that appear.

3. **Set Up Your Space**

    o   **Name Your Space** – Choose a clear, descriptive title that tells users what the conversation is about.

    o   **Select Topics** – X allows you to pick up to three topics to help users discover your Space.

    o   **Enable Recording (Optional)** – You can choose to record your Space for later playback.

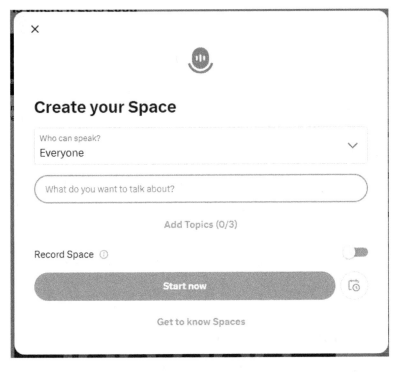

4. **Customize Speaker Permissions**

   o Decide who can speak:

      ▪ **Everyone** – Any listener can request to speak.

      ▪ **People You Follow** – Only those you follow can request to speak.

      ▪ **Invite-Only** – Only people you manually invite can speak.

5. **Go Live**

   o Tap **"Start Your Space"** to begin.

   o Once live, you can invite people, manage speakers, and moderate discussions.

Managing Your Space as a Host

Once your Space is live, you have several tools to control the conversation effectively.

- Inviting People to Join

- **Share via Tweet** – Promote your Space by tweeting a link.

- **Send Direct Invites** – You can send invitations via DMs.

- **Pin Your Space to Your Profile** – This makes it easier for your followers to find and join.

- Adding and Managing Speakers

- **Approve Speaker Requests** – Listeners can request to speak; you decide who gets access.

- **Manually Invite Speakers** – Tap on a user's profile and select "Invite to Speak."

- **Mute or Remove Speakers** – As a host, you can mute disruptive speakers or remove them if necessary.

- Engaging Your Audience

- Encourage listeners to use emojis to react in real-time.

- Ask open-ended questions to spark discussions.

- Acknowledge new listeners by greeting them when they join.

- Ending Your Space

- When you're ready to close the Space, tap the **End** button.

- If you recorded the session, X will provide an option to share the recording.

---

3. How to Join a Space

If you want to listen to or participate in an existing Space, follow these steps.

Finding a Space to Join

- **Explore Tab** – X features live and upcoming Spaces on the Explore page.

- **Following Hosts** – If someone you follow is hosting a Space, you'll see it at the top of your timeline.

- **Direct Invitations** – Hosts can send links to Spaces via tweets or DMs.

Joining as a Listener

1. **Tap on the Space**

   o Click on the Space title or the purple circle at the top of your timeline.

2. **Listen Anonymously or Interact**

   o You can stay as a silent listener or react with emojis.

3. **Request to Speak (Optional)**

   o If you want to contribute to the conversation, tap the **Request to Speak** button.

   o The host will approve or deny your request.

---

4. Best Practices for Hosting a Successful Space

To maximize engagement and ensure a smooth conversation, follow these tips:

Plan Ahead

- Choose a relevant and engaging topic.
- Announce your Space in advance to attract listeners.

Moderate Effectively

- Establish ground rules for discussions.
- Remove disruptive participants if needed.

Encourage Participation

- Ask questions and encourage audience input.
- Use polls and interactive elements to engage listeners.

Promote Your Space

- Tweet about your upcoming Space to generate interest.
- Collaborate with other creators to expand your reach.

Conclusion

Hosting and joining Spaces on X provides a powerful way to engage with your audience, discuss trending topics, and build your brand. Whether you're looking to share knowledge, network with industry experts, or simply have fun conversations, Spaces offers a unique real-time experience. By following best practices and leveraging the platform's tools, you can create meaningful and impactful discussions that resonate with your audience.

4.2.2 Moderating and Managing Listeners

Introduction

X (formerly Twitter) Spaces is a powerful tool for live audio conversations, enabling users to host discussions, interviews, Q&A sessions, and more. However, managing a live audience in a Space requires strong moderation skills to maintain a productive and respectful conversation. Without proper moderation, discussions can easily go off track, leading to disruptive participants, spam, or even hostile interactions.

In this section, we will cover essential strategies for moderating and managing listeners in Spaces, including setting ground rules, handling disruptive participants, encouraging engagement, and utilizing moderation tools effectively.

1. Understanding the Role of a Moderator in Spaces

Moderators in Spaces serve multiple roles:

- **Facilitators** – They guide the conversation, ensuring that speakers stay on topic and that discussions remain meaningful.

- **Gatekeepers** – They control who speaks and manage audience participation.

- **Problem-Solvers** – They handle disruptions, spam, or inappropriate behavior.

- **Engagement Drivers** – They encourage audience interaction and ensure a lively, balanced discussion.

A good moderator creates a welcoming environment where listeners feel comfortable participating while maintaining order and focus.

2. Preparing for a Well-Moderated Space

Setting Clear Expectations

Before starting your Space, set clear expectations for participation. You can do this by:

- Stating the **purpose** of the Space at the beginning.

- Explaining any **ground rules** (e.g., no hate speech, respect all participants, stay on topic).

- Letting participants know how they can request to speak and how questions will be handled.

Selecting Co-Hosts and Moderators

Managing a large audience alone can be challenging. X allows hosts to add **co-hosts**, who can help with moderation tasks. Consider selecting:

- **A trusted co-host** – Someone familiar with the topic who can help manage discussions.

- **A technical moderator** – Someone who monitors spam and manages speaker requests.

Co-hosts can:
✓ Approve or deny speaker requests
✓ Mute or remove disruptive speakers
✓ Pin important tweets to the conversation

Structuring the Discussion

To keep the conversation smooth, plan your discussion flow in advance:

1. **Introduction:** Welcome listeners and set expectations.

2. **Main Discussion:** Cover key topics with guest speakers or panelists.

3. **Audience Interaction:** Open the floor for Q&A or listener contributions.

4. **Conclusion:** Summarize key points and encourage follow-up actions.

By having a clear structure, you can avoid long silences, off-topic discussions, or chaotic conversations.

3. Managing Listener Participation

Encouraging Constructive Engagement

Listeners contribute to the success of a Space. To keep engagement high and meaningful:

- Ask **open-ended questions** to prompt discussion.

- Acknowledge listener comments and reactions (emoji reactions can show agreement).

- Encourage **respectful debates** while steering conversations back on track if needed.

- Use **polls or pinned tweets** to get quick audience feedback.

Handling Speaker Requests

X Spaces allows listeners to request speaking roles. As a moderator, you should:

✓ **Vet speaker requests** – Approve those who seem relevant to the topic.
✓ **Prioritize active listeners** – Those who have engaged in the chat or reacted positively.
✓ **Limit speakers per session** – Too many speakers can make the conversation hard to follow.

If a listener speaks off-topic, politely guide them back:
"That's an interesting point, but let's keep the focus on [topic]. We'll revisit this later."

Managing Microphone Etiquette

To maintain audio quality and avoid disruptions:

- Ask speakers to **mute their mic** when not speaking.

- Mute background noise if a speaker forgets to mute themselves.

- Encourage **brief and concise responses** to keep the conversation flowing.

If a speaker dominates the discussion, step in politely:
"Thank you for sharing! Let's hear from others as well."

4. Handling Disruptions and Trolls

Recognizing and Addressing Disruptive Behavior

Some listeners may enter your Space to troll, disrupt, or spam. Common issues include:

- **Spamming** – Repeating messages or promoting unrelated content.

- **Interrupting speakers** – Constantly talking over others.

- **Hate speech or offensive language** – Violating community guidelines.

If you notice disruptive behavior, act quickly.

Using Moderation Tools Effectively

X Spaces provides tools to control disruptions:

✅ **Mute speakers** – Prevents interruptions without removing them.
✅ **Remove from speaking role** – If a participant ignores warnings.
✅ **Block and report** – If someone is being offensive or violating platform policies.

To remove a participant:

1. Tap on their profile.

2. Select "Remove from Space" or "Block and Report."

3. Provide a reason (optional).

It's best to give a warning before taking action:
"Let's keep the conversation respectful. If disruptive behavior continues, we may have to remove you."

5. Enhancing Listener Experience

Creating an Inclusive Environment

Ensure that all participants feel welcome by:

- Using **inclusive language** and avoiding jargon.

- Encouraging **diverse voices** – Invite speakers from different backgrounds.

- Providing **content summaries** for late joiners.

Using Pinned Tweets to Enhance Discussions

Pin tweets related to the discussion topic, such as:

- A **summary thread** of key points.

- A **link to a website, blog, or resource** for more information.

- A **live poll** for audience engagement.

Pinned tweets can help keep listeners informed and engaged.

Ending the Space on a Strong Note

When wrapping up the session:

- Thank your audience for participating.

- Summarize the main takeaways.

- Encourage listeners to follow you for future discussions.

- Ask for **feedback** – "What topics would you like to hear next?"

Ending with a **call to action** helps retain audience engagement for future Spaces.

Conclusion

Moderating and managing listeners in X Spaces requires a mix of preparation, active listening, and quick decision-making. By setting clear expectations, encouraging meaningful interactions, and handling disruptions professionally, you can create a valuable and engaging experience for your audience.

As you gain experience in hosting Spaces, refining your moderation skills will help you build a stronger, more interactive community. Whether you're running a casual discussion, a professional panel, or a marketing event, good moderation ensures a positive and productive live audio experience.

4.3 Lists: Organizing Your Feed

4.3.1 Creating and Managing Lists

Introduction to X (Twitter) Lists

In the fast-paced world of social media, keeping track of important content, accounts, and discussions can be challenging. X (Twitter) Lists offer a powerful solution by allowing users to organize accounts into curated feeds. These Lists help streamline your experience, ensuring you see the most relevant updates without unnecessary distractions. Whether you want to track industry leaders, follow specific topics, or organize your personal and professional networks, Lists can enhance your ability to navigate X efficiently.

This section will guide you through the process of creating, managing, and optimizing Lists on X, helping you make the most of this underutilized feature.

←   **Suggested Lists**

Choose your Lists

When you follow a List, you'll be able to quickly keep up with the experts on
what you care about most.

Discover new Lists

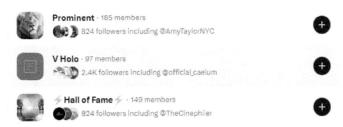

Prominent · 185 members
824 followers including @AmyTaylorNYC

V Holo · 97 members
2.4K followers including @official_caelum

⚡ **Hall of Fame** ⚡ · 149 members
824 followers including @TheCinephiler

1. Understanding X (Twitter) Lists

X (Twitter) Lists are essentially curated feeds consisting of selected accounts. Instead of scrolling through your entire timeline, which includes posts from all the people you follow, Lists allow you to view posts from specific groups of accounts.

Benefits of Using Lists:

- **Improved Content Organization:** Easily separate different interests such as news, business, entertainment, or hobbies.

- **Better Focus:** Avoid clutter by narrowing down your feed to only essential voices.

- **Enhanced Engagement:** Engage more effectively with industry leaders, clients, or communities without missing key updates.

- **News Tracking:** Stay updated on real-time developments in specific sectors, such as technology, finance, or sports.

- **Competitor Monitoring:** Follow competitors without actually following them publicly.

Lists can be either **public** or **private** (explained further in Section 4.3.2). Public Lists are visible to everyone and can be followed by others, while private Lists are only accessible to you.

2. How to Create a List on X (Twitter)

Creating a List is simple and can be done on both desktop and mobile devices.

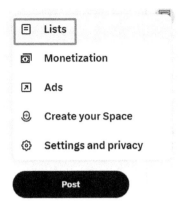

Steps to Create a List on Desktop:

1. **Open X (Twitter)** and log in to your account.

2. **Click on "Lists"** in the left-hand menu.

3. **Select the "New List" button** (usually a plus sign or "Create new List" option).

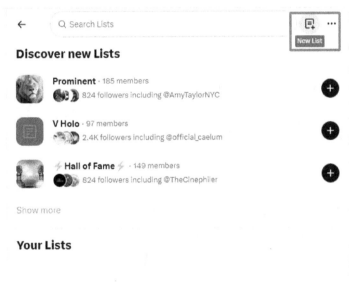

4. **Enter a List Name** (e.g., "Tech News," "Marketing Experts," or "Favorite Creators").

5. **Write a Description** (optional but recommended for better organization).

6. **Choose the Privacy Setting:**

- o **Public List:** Anyone can see and follow it.
- o **Private List:** Only you can access and view it.

7. **Add Accounts to the List:** Search for and select the users you want to include.

8. **Save and Confirm.**

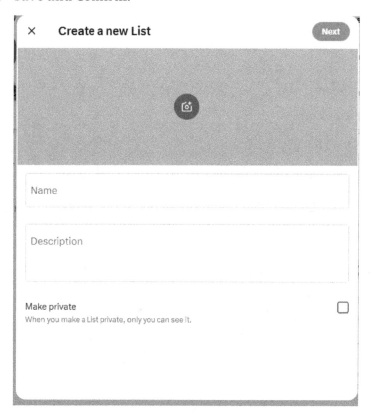

Steps to Create a List on Mobile (iOS/Android):

1. Open the **X (Twitter) app** and tap on your profile picture.

2. Scroll down and tap on **"Lists."**

3. Tap the **"+" (New List)** button.

4. Enter a **List Name and Description** (optional).

5. Select the **privacy setting (public or private).**

6. Tap **"Add members"** and search for the accounts you want to include.

7. Tap **"Done"** and save the List.

Once created, you can access this List anytime to view tweets only from the selected members.

3. Adding and Removing Accounts from Lists

Once you have created a List, you can modify it by adding or removing accounts at any time.

To Add Accounts to an Existing List:

1. Go to the profile of the account you want to add.

2. Click on the three-dot menu (More Options).

3. Select **"Add/remove from Lists."**

4. Choose the List(s) you want to add the account to.

5. Save your selection.

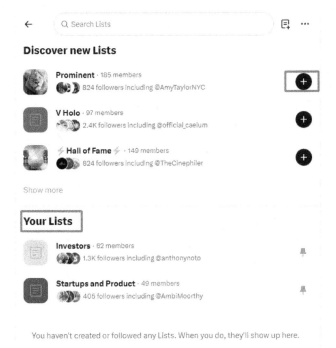

To Remove Accounts from a List:

1. Go to your **Lists** section and open the List.

2. Click on the **"Members"** tab.

3. Find the account you want to remove.

4. Click the **three-dot menu** next to their name.

5. Select **"Remove from List."**

This helps you refine and adjust your Lists over time based on relevance and engagement.

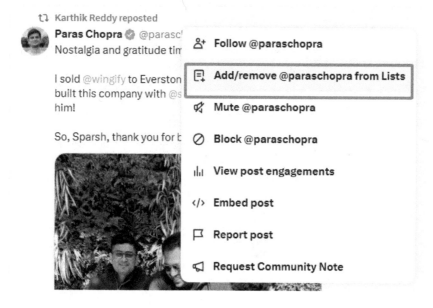

---

4. Managing and Customizing Lists

After creating a List, you can manage it by renaming it, changing its privacy settings, or even deleting it if necessary.

Editing a List:

1. Navigate to the **Lists** section.

2. Select the List you want to edit.

3. Click on the **"Edit"** button (often represented by a pencil icon).

4. Modify the **name, description, or privacy settings.**

5. Click **Save Changes.**

Deleting a List:

1. Open the List you want to remove.

2. Click on the **three-dot menu.**

3. Select **"Delete List"** and confirm your choice.

Be careful when deleting Lists, as this action is irreversible.

5. Using Lists to Improve Your Experience on X (Twitter)

Lists are not just a tool for organizing accounts; they can significantly enhance your experience and efficiency on the platform.

Best Ways to Use Lists Effectively:

- **Follow Industry Trends:** Create Lists of industry experts, journalists, and influencers to stay updated on the latest news.

- **Engage with Communities:** Build Lists of active users in specific communities to join discussions easily.

- **Separate Personal and Professional Networks:** Maintain different Lists for friends, family, colleagues, and business contacts.

- **Track Competitors and Brands:** Keep an eye on competitors or brands without following them publicly.

- **Save Content for Later:** Create Lists of content creators or educators whose insights you want to revisit regularly.

Example List Categories You Can Create:

- **"Tech News"** – For following top tech publications and analysts.

- **"Marketing Gurus"** – To stay updated with digital marketing strategies.

- **"Startup Founders"** – To engage with entrepreneurs and innovators.

- **"Freelancers & Creatives"** – To connect with designers, writers, and artists.

- **"Financial Markets"** – To track stock market and investment discussions.

---

6. Following and Subscribing to Public Lists

Besides creating your own Lists, you can also **follow public Lists** created by others. This is a great way to access well-curated content without having to manually find and add accounts.

How to Follow a Public List:

1. Go to an account that has public Lists (such as news organizations or industry leaders).

2. Click on the **"Lists"** tab on their profile.

3. Browse through available public Lists.

4. Click on the List you're interested in.

5. Select **"Follow"** to add it to your Lists section.

This allows you to access niche content without cluttering your main feed.

Conclusion

Lists are an incredibly powerful yet underutilized feature on X (Twitter). By effectively creating, managing, and utilizing Lists, you can gain better control over your content consumption, improve engagement, and stay updated with relevant discussions. Whether for personal organization, professional networking, or industry tracking, Lists provide a structured way to enhance your social media experience.

By implementing the strategies outlined in this section, you can turn X (Twitter) into a more efficient and personalized platform tailored to your needs.

4.3.2 Public vs. Private Lists

X (Twitter) Lists are a valuable tool for organizing your feed, and they come with the flexibility to be either public or private. Understanding the difference between these two types of Lists and when to use them can enhance your social media experience and ensure you are making the most of X's organizational features. This section will explore the advantages and practical applications of both **public** and **private** Lists, helping you decide which is best suited to your needs.

1. What Are Public Lists?

A **public List** is visible to everyone on X (Twitter). When you create a public List, it can be followed by any user, not just those who are part of the List. Public Lists are ideal for sharing collections of accounts that you want others to discover or follow. For example, you may want to create a List of top industry leaders in your field and share it with your followers or the broader community.

Benefits of Public Lists

1. **Visibility and Shareability:** Public Lists allow you to share curated content with a larger audience. Whether you are a business, influencer, or enthusiast, public Lists can help you establish your expertise by highlighting key voices in your industry.

2. **Building a Community:** By creating a public List, you encourage others to follow along. If your List features valuable insights or a collection of relevant accounts, it may attract new followers who share similar interests.

3. **Engagement and Recognition:** Public Lists can boost engagement with accounts featured in the List, as they may see themselves included and interact with the curator or others within the List. This recognition can foster more connections and collaborations.

4. **Discoverability:** Public Lists increase your visibility and can be found through searches, meaning others may discover your profile by exploring the Lists you've created. Many users follow public Lists created by others to stay informed on specific topics or interests.

5. **Curating Expert Opinions:** If you're a professional or thought leader, creating public Lists is an excellent way to position yourself as a curator of quality content. You can build a reputation for aggregating the best information from reliable sources.

How to Create a Public List

Creating a public List on X is straightforward:

1. **Navigate to your Lists section** on X (Twitter).

2. Click the **"Create a new List"** button.

3. Name your List and provide a short description that indicates what it's about.

4. Select the **Public** option under privacy settings.

5. Add the accounts you want to feature in the List.

6. **Save and share** your List, either by promoting it in your tweets or sharing it directly with others.

After creating a public List, others will be able to follow it, and it will be visible in their Lists feed.

---

2. What Are Private Lists?

A **private List**, on the other hand, is only visible to you. No one else can see the accounts included in the List, and no one can follow the List unless you specifically allow them to do so. Private Lists are ideal for organizing your feed in a way that maintains privacy, whether for personal use or sensitive business-related content.

Benefits of Private Lists

1. **Confidentiality and Privacy:** Private Lists ensure that the accounts you track remain hidden from others. This is especially useful if you're tracking competitors, personal contacts, or sensitive information that you don't want to share publicly.

2. **Personal Organization:** Private Lists allow you to categorize accounts in a way that makes sense to you without anyone else knowing. For example, you could create a private List for friends and family, a separate one for work colleagues, or even one for certain content you want to check later.

3. **Monitoring Competitors:** If you're in business or a competitive industry, you can create private Lists to monitor competitors without them knowing. This helps you keep track of their activities and trends without drawing attention to the fact that you're following them.

4. **Avoiding Overexposure:** By using private Lists, you can curate information without the pressure of others seeing what you're tracking. This ensures that your

content organization remains discreet, which can be valuable for those who prefer a more private social media experience.

5. **Zero Pressure Engagement:** Since private Lists are for your eyes only, there is no need to worry about how the people you're following will react or engage. You can freely add or remove accounts without worrying about making things public.

How to Create a Private List

Creating a private List is very similar to creating a public List, but with a key difference in privacy settings:

1. **Navigate to your Lists section** on X (Twitter).

2. Click the **"Create a new List"** button.

3. Name your List and add a description, if you wish.

4. Select the **Private** option under privacy settings.

5. Add the accounts you wish to include in the List.

6. Save and close the List creation window.

Once created, private Lists remain entirely under your control. Only you will see which accounts are included, and you are free to update them as you see fit.

3. Choosing Between Public and Private Lists

Knowing when to use a public List versus a private List depends on your objectives and the type of content you're curating. Both types of Lists offer distinct advantages, and there are different circumstances in which each is most appropriate. Below are some considerations that can help you decide which type of List to create.

When to Use Public Lists:

- **Promoting Industry Expertise:** If you are a professional, business owner, or influencer who wants to position yourself as a thought leader, creating public Lists can help you build a reputation as a curator of relevant content.

- **Sharing Knowledge:** If you're actively sharing valuable resources, a public List is a great way to make those resources more accessible to others, whether in your field or community.

- **Building Community:** Public Lists can help you grow your network and attract like-minded individuals or potential collaborators.

- **Tracking Trends:** Public Lists allow others to track trends or specific conversations, which can be helpful for discussions on popular topics, breaking news, or industry developments.

When to Use Private Lists:

- **Personal Organization:** If you prefer to keep your feed organized for your own use—such as keeping track of friends, family, or interests—private Lists offer a discreet way to categorize your timeline.

- **Competitor Analysis:** If you're tracking competitors or sensitive industry information, private Lists are the best option since they allow you to monitor trends and activities without revealing your intentions.

- **Sensitive Projects:** For work-related projects, private Lists allow you to follow certain accounts for internal purposes, such as team members or collaborators, without exposing them to external audiences.

- **Reducing Pressure:** If you don't want anyone to know which accounts you are following or which content you're interested in, private Lists provide the necessary privacy.

4. Managing Both Public and Private Lists

Both types of Lists offer flexibility, but it's important to manage them carefully. A cluttered or poorly organized List can quickly lose its value, whether it's public or private. Here are some tips for managing both public and private Lists:

1. Organize with Clear Categories:

Whether public or private, Lists should have clear and meaningful names and descriptions. This makes it easier to find relevant accounts and provides context to others if you are sharing your Lists.

2. Regularly Update Your Lists:

Don't let Lists become outdated. Check and update your Lists by adding new accounts or removing inactive or irrelevant ones. This ensures that your Lists remain valuable over time.

3. Monitor Your Privacy Settings:

Remember that any changes made to the privacy of a List can affect its visibility. Double-check whether a List is public or private before making updates or sharing it.

4. Use Lists for Different Purposes:

As you create more Lists, think of different use cases for each one. Public Lists can be for audience engagement, while private Lists can help you stay organized or track competitors discreetly.

Conclusion

Understanding the difference between public and private Lists is essential for maximizing the organizational potential of X (Twitter). Both offer unique advantages depending on your goals, whether you want to share curated content with a wider audience or keep your feed neatly organized for personal use. By using both types of Lists strategically, you can enhance your X experience, stay focused on what matters most, and better manage your social media activity.

4.4 Communities: Engaging in Group Discussions

4.4.1 Joining and Participating in Communities

Introduction to Communities on X (Twitter)

In the ever-expanding world of social media, finding like-minded individuals and engaging in group discussions has never been easier. X (Twitter) Communities offer users the opportunity to come together in a more focused and intimate setting. These communities are designed to connect people who share common interests, passions, or goals, allowing them to interact, share ideas, and engage in meaningful conversations.

Communities are a unique feature that fosters collaboration and knowledge-sharing, helping users build stronger relationships around shared topics. Whether you're interested in technology, sports, politics, or entertainment, there's a community on X (Twitter) for virtually every interest. In this section, we'll explore how you can join and participate in communities, enhancing your social media experience and allowing you to connect with others who share your passions.

1. Understanding X (Twitter) Communities

X (Twitter) Communities are dedicated spaces within the platform where users can gather around a specific topic, interest, or activity. Unlike the open conversations in your main feed, communities provide a more controlled environment, where members can post, reply, and share content specifically within the context of the community's theme.

Key Features of X (Twitter) Communities:

- **Focused Discussions:** Communities allow for more relevant, niche conversations than general public timelines.

- **Private and Inclusive:** Communities can be private or public. Private communities require an invitation to join, while public communities are open to anyone.

- **Curated Content:** Posts in communities are filtered to match the community's focus, ensuring the content shared is relevant to all members.

- **Moderation:** Community admins and moderators help keep discussions on-topic and respectful, ensuring that the environment is welcoming and engaging.

Communities on X (Twitter) provide a powerful tool for users who want to dive deeper into specific subjects and engage with others who have similar interests.

---

2. How to Join a Community on X (Twitter)

Joining a community on X (Twitter) is a straightforward process, but there are certain steps and considerations to keep in mind.

Steps to Join a Community on X (Twitter):

1. **Log In to Your X (Twitter) Account:** Open your X account and ensure you are logged in with the profile that you wish to use for community engagement.

2. **Explore the Communities Tab:** On both desktop and mobile, navigate to the **Communities** section. This can be found in the side menu on the desktop version or under your profile icon on the mobile app.

3. **Browse Available Communities:** You can either browse through suggested communities based on your interests or use the search bar to find a specific community related to your interests (e.g., "digital marketing," "sports enthusiasts," "book lovers").

4. **Request to Join or Follow a Community:**

   o **Public Communities:** These are open to all. To join, simply click on the community and select **"Join"**.

   o **Private Communities:** These require an invitation. You can request to join by clicking **"Request to Join"** or waiting for an invitation from an admin or existing member.

5. **Wait for Approval (If Needed):** If you are trying to join a private community, you may need to wait for approval from the community's moderators before you can participate.

Once you're a member, you can start engaging with posts, conversations, and other members.

3. How to Participate in Communities

Joining a community is only the first step; active participation is what truly enhances your experience. Engaging with others in communities can help you gain valuable insights, build relationships, and become an influential member of the group.

Posting in a Community:

Once you're a member, you can contribute to the community by posting relevant content. Here are some tips to help you post effectively:

- **Stay on Topic:** Communities are usually centered around specific themes. Ensure your posts are aligned with the community's focus to maintain relevance.

- **Be Respectful:** Follow the community's guidelines and respect other members' opinions. Positive and constructive interactions help create a healthy environment for everyone.

- **Share Value:** Post content that adds value to the conversation. Share useful articles, thought-provoking questions, or personal experiences that contribute to the topic at hand.

Engaging with Posts in the Community:

In addition to posting your own content, actively engage with the posts shared by others. Liking, retweeting, and replying to other members' posts can spark conversation and deepen connections.

- **Like and Share Posts:** If you find a post interesting, like it to show appreciation. If it resonates with you or offers valuable information, share it with your followers.

- **Reply Thoughtfully:** When responding to other members' posts, make sure your replies are respectful, well-thought-out, and relevant. Ask questions, provide feedback, or share your own experiences to contribute meaningfully to the conversation.

- **Tag Members:** If you want to engage with a specific member or bring their attention to a post, you can tag them using the @ symbol. This can help foster direct conversations and build relationships.

Participating in Community Polls or Events:

Many communities host polls, live chats, or events to keep members engaged. These are great opportunities for participation and can help you stay informed and involved.

- **Respond to Polls:** Communities may run polls to gather opinions or feedback from members. Participate in these to share your thoughts and contribute to the overall group conversation.

- **Join Events or Live Sessions:** Some communities host live audio chats or events that you can join. These are perfect for real-time interactions and discussions.

4. Best Practices for Engaging in Communities

To truly get the most out of your experience in communities, here are some best practices to keep in mind:

Be Consistent but Not Overbearing:

Engage consistently with the community to stay visible and build relationships, but avoid overposting or spamming the group with excessive content. Quality matters more than quantity.

Listen and Learn:

Communities are not just about talking, but also about listening. Take time to read other members' posts and learn from their experiences and insights. This can deepen your understanding of the topic and make your own contributions more valuable.

Respect the Community Guidelines:

Every community has its own set of rules and guidelines to ensure the space remains welcoming and productive. Make sure you are familiar with these guidelines and follow them in your interactions.

Ask Questions and Offer Help:

Communities thrive on mutual help. Don't hesitate to ask questions if you need clarification on a topic, and be generous in offering your knowledge to others. Providing help is a great way to establish yourself as a valuable member of the community.

Engage with a Positive Attitude:

Stay positive and supportive in your interactions. Be encouraging when others share ideas, and avoid negative or hostile comments. A friendly and helpful attitude will make you more approachable and contribute to a better group atmosphere.

5. Benefits of Active Participation in Communities

By actively participating in X (Twitter) Communities, you'll experience several key benefits that can enhance both your personal and professional life.

Networking Opportunities:

Communities offer a unique opportunity to network with people who share similar interests or professional goals. Building connections with members of your communities can lead to new friendships, collaborations, and career opportunities.

Learning and Knowledge Sharing:

Being part of a community allows you to learn from others and stay updated on the latest trends, tools, and ideas in your area of interest. Engaging with experts and thought leaders can also help you grow and develop new skills.

Building Your Reputation:

As you consistently contribute valuable content and insights to a community, you'll build a reputation as a knowledgeable and reliable member. This can increase your credibility and visibility both within the community and beyond.

Personal Growth:

Communities allow you to engage in thoughtful, meaningful conversations that can broaden your perspectives and challenge your thinking. The exchange of ideas in a supportive environment encourages personal growth and self-improvement.

Conclusion

X (Twitter) Communities offer a dynamic and engaging way to interact with like-minded individuals and dive deeper into the topics that matter most to you. Joining and actively participating in communities not only helps you stay informed but also allows you to build meaningful connections, contribute valuable insights, and grow your online presence. By following the steps outlined in this section, you can fully immerse yourself in the vibrant world of communities on X and take your social media experience to the next level.

4.4.2 Creating Your Own Community

Introduction

Building your own community on X (Twitter) is a great way to connect like-minded individuals, foster discussions, and create a space where people can share ideas around a specific topic. Whether you want to establish a professional network, grow a fanbase, or facilitate niche discussions, a well-managed community can significantly enhance engagement and collaboration.

This section will guide you through the process of creating, managing, and growing a successful X (Twitter) Community.

1. What is an X (Twitter) Community?

An X (Twitter) Community is a dedicated space where users can gather around a shared interest or topic. Unlike the main timeline, which is open to all followers, Community posts are only visible to its members.

Benefits of Creating a Community:

- **Focused Discussions:** Keep conversations relevant and free from unrelated content.

- **Stronger Engagement:** Build deeper connections with members who share your interests.

- **Community Moderation:** Set rules and control who can join and participate.

- **Networking Opportunities:** Bring together industry professionals, hobbyists, or enthusiasts.

- **Content Curation:** Create a specialized hub for high-quality discussions.

2. How to Create an X (Twitter) Community

Creating a Community on X (Twitter) is a straightforward process. Follow these steps to set up your own group:

Step 1: Access the Communities Feature

1. Log into your X (Twitter) account.

2. Navigate to the **Communities** tab from the main menu.

3. Click on the **"+"** (Create a Community) button.

Step 2: Set Up Basic Community Details

You will need to fill out some important information:

- **Community Name:** Choose a unique and relevant name. Example: "Digital Marketing Hub" or "AI and Tech Enthusiasts."

- **Description:** Write a brief summary explaining the purpose of your Community. Example: "A space for marketers to share trends, insights, and strategies in digital advertising."

- **Category:** Select the most relevant category (e.g., Business, Technology, Lifestyle).

Step 3: Set Privacy and Membership Settings

X (Twitter) allows you to define who can join and participate in your Community:

- **Open Community:** Anyone can join and post.

- **Restricted Community:** Anyone can request to join, but approval is required.

- **Invite-Only Community:** Only those invited by moderators can join.

Step 4: Define Community Rules

Every Community needs clear guidelines to maintain respectful and productive discussions. Consider including rules such as:

- **Stay on topic:** Keep discussions relevant to the Community's purpose.

- **No hate speech or harassment:** Foster a respectful environment.

- **No spam or self-promotion:** Prevent excessive advertising.

Once these details are finalized, click **"Create"** to launch your Community.

3. Managing and Moderating Your Community

Once your Community is live, you need to manage it effectively to encourage engagement and maintain a positive environment.

Appointing Moderators

As a Community grows, managing discussions alone can be challenging. You can appoint **moderators** to help oversee activities, approve new members, and enforce rules.

Steps to Add a Moderator:

1. Go to your Community settings.

2. Click on **"Manage Moderators"** under Community roles.

3. Search for the user and select **"Add as Moderator."**

Approving and Removing Members

If your Community has restricted or invite-only access, you'll need to **approve new members** manually.

- Approve **active and engaged users** who align with your Community's goals.

- Remove **spam accounts or disruptive users** who violate rules.

To remove a member:

1. Go to the **Members** tab.

2. Click the three-dot menu next to their name.

3. Select **"Remove from Community."**

Encouraging Engagement

To keep your Community active and engaging, consider the following strategies:

- **Post Regularly:** Share interesting content, news, and questions to spark discussions.

- **Ask Questions:** Encourage members to share their opinions and experiences.

- **Feature Member Contributions:** Highlight insightful posts to motivate participation.

- **Host Community Events:** Organize Q&A sessions, Twitter Spaces, or themed discussions.

4. Growing Your Community

A thriving Community requires a steady flow of new, engaged members. Here's how to attract more people:

1. Promote Your Community on X (Twitter)

- **Pin a tweet** on your profile with an invitation to join.
- **Use relevant hashtags** when posting about your Community.
- **Encourage members to invite others** who may be interested.

2. Collaborate with Influencers and Experts

- Partner with well-known users in your niche to attract their audience.
- Invite guest contributors to share insights within the Community.

3. Share Exclusive Content

- Offer **early access to industry insights, tips, or discussions.**
- Conduct **giveaways or special Q&A sessions** for members.

5. Maintaining a Healthy and Active Community

Building a Community is just the beginning—maintaining engagement and fostering a positive atmosphere is essential.

1. Monitor Activity Regularly

- Keep an eye on discussions to prevent spam or inappropriate content.
- Engage with members by liking, commenting, or resharing posts.

2. Enforce Community Rules Fairly

- Be consistent with rule enforcement to maintain credibility.
- Give **warnings for minor infractions** and remove repeat offenders.

3. Keep the Community Evolving

- Gather member feedback on improvements.

- Adjust guidelines as needed to accommodate new trends or topics.

Conclusion

Creating and managing an X (Twitter) Community can be an excellent way to build a highly engaged audience around a shared interest. With careful planning, effective moderation, and consistent engagement, your Community can become a valuable space for meaningful discussions and networking.

By following the steps outlined in this section, you'll be able to **successfully launch, grow, and maintain a thriving Community** on X (Twitter).

4.5 Polls and Interactive Features

4.5.1 How to Create a Poll

Polls are a powerful interactive feature on X (Twitter) that allow users to gather opinions, conduct surveys, and engage their audience in a dynamic way. Whether you want to make decisions, spark conversations, or just entertain your followers, polls can be an effective tool. In this section, we'll explore everything you need to know about creating and optimizing polls on X.

Understanding X (Twitter) Polls

A poll on X consists of a question and multiple answer options, allowing users to vote on their preferred choice. Polls are especially useful for businesses, influencers, and general users who want to encourage engagement and interaction.

Key Features of X Polls:

- Users can add **two to four** response options.

- Polls remain open for a **minimum of five minutes** and a **maximum of seven days**.

- Once a user votes, they can't change their selection.

- Poll results are displayed in percentages, and only the poll creator can see who voted for which option.

- Polls can be created on both **mobile** and **desktop** versions of X.

Step-by-Step Guide to Creating a Poll

Creating a poll on X is a straightforward process. Below are the step-by-step instructions for setting up an effective poll:

Step 1: Open the Post (Tweet) Composer

To create a poll, you need to start a new post (tweet). This can be done by clicking on the **"+"** icon or the **"Tweet"** button on the X platform.

Step 2: Select the Poll Option

Once the tweet composer is open, look for the **icon** representing the poll feature. Click on it to enable the poll creation interface.

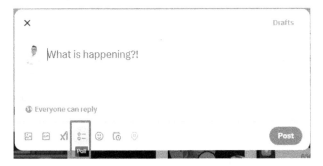

Step 3: Write Your Poll Question

In the main text box, type out your question. A good poll question should be:

- **Clear**: Avoid vague wording that could lead to confusion.

- **Concise**: Keep it short so users can quickly understand the choices.

- **Engaging**: Make it interesting enough to encourage participation.

Example Poll Questions:

- *Which social media platform do you use the most?*

- *What's the best way to start the day?*

- *Which feature do you want X to improve?*

Step 4: Add Poll Choices

You can include between **two and four** answer options. Each option has a **25-character limit**, so keep the choices short and meaningful.

Example Choices for a Poll on Social Media Usage:

- Facebook
- Instagram
- TikTok
- X (Twitter)

Step 5: Set the Poll Duration

By default, polls last for **24 hours**, but you can adjust this timeframe. X allows you to choose any duration between **five minutes and seven days**.

Recommended Poll Duration:

- **5 minutes – 1 hour**: Ideal for live events and quick feedback.

- **24 hours**: Best for general engagement and daily audience interaction.

- **3–7 days**: Useful for long-term surveys and strategic research.

Step 6: Add Context (Optional)

Although polls stand alone, adding a bit of context can increase engagement. You can:

- Include a **hashtag** (e.g., #MarketingPoll) to attract a wider audience.

- Mention a **call-to-action** (e.g., "Vote now!" or "Let us know your thoughts!").

- Tag relevant **users or brands** to encourage more participation.

Step 7: Post Your Poll

Once everything is set up, click **"Post"** to publish your poll. It will appear on your followers' feeds, and they can start voting immediately.

Optimizing Polls for Maximum Engagement

To get the most out of your polls, follow these best practices:

1. Choose Relevant Topics

Make sure your poll topic is interesting and relevant to your audience. Popular topics include:

- Industry trends (e.g., *What's the most exciting tech innovation of 2025?*)

- Personal preferences (e.g., *Do you prefer coffee or tea?*)

- Community decisions (e.g., *Which book should we review next?*)

2. Keep It Simple

Avoid overly complex questions. Instead of:
✗ *If you could have dinner with one of these historical figures, who would it be and why?*
Try:
✓ *Who is the most inspiring historical figure?*

3. Leverage Timeliness

Tie your poll to **current events, holidays, or trending topics**. This increases the chances of it appearing in search results and trending discussions.

4. Use Hashtags and Mentions

Adding relevant **hashtags** (e.g., #Poll #Marketing) helps reach a broader audience. Tagging influencers or brands can also encourage them to share your poll.

5. Follow Up with a Discussion

After the poll closes, keep the conversation going by:

- **Sharing the results** with insights.
- **Asking a follow-up question** to continue engagement.
- **Tagging voters** (if appropriate) to start a discussion.

Example Follow-Up Post:

"Thanks for voting! 60% of you prefer Instagram over TikTok. What features do you love the most?"

Examples of Effective Polls on X (Twitter)

To inspire your own polls, here are some effective examples from different industries:

For Businesses:

💡 *Which new feature would you like to see in our app?*

- Dark Mode
- Faster Load Time
- More Customization

For Influencers & Content Creators:

✏️ *What type of content should I create next?*

- Q&A Session
- Behind-the-Scenes
- Product Reviews

For Personal Users:

📣 *What's the best pizza topping?*

- Pepperoni
- Mushrooms
- Pineapple
- Extra Cheese

Common Mistakes to Avoid

✘ Using Biased or Leading Questions

Avoid questions that push users toward a specific answer. Instead of:
✘ *Do you agree that pineapple doesn't belong on pizza?*
Try:
✓ *How do you feel about pineapple on pizza?*

✘ Making Polls Too Long or Complicated

Stick to short, easy-to-understand questions and responses.

✘ Not Promoting Your Poll

If you have a smaller audience, **pin your poll** to your profile or **retweet it** to maximize participation.

Final Thoughts

Polls on X (Twitter) are a fantastic way to engage your audience, gather insights, and create interactive content. By following best practices and avoiding common mistakes, you can create compelling polls that spark conversations and boost engagement.

Now that you've learned how to create effective polls, the next section will cover **best practices for poll engagement**, helping you maximize participation and interaction on your polls.

4.5.2 Best Practices for Engagement

Interactive features like **polls** play a significant role in increasing engagement on X (Twitter). They provide a quick and easy way for users to participate in conversations, give feedback, and interact with content without requiring much effort. However, simply creating a poll isn't enough—you need to **strategically design, time, and promote it** to maximize engagement.

In this section, we'll explore **the best practices for using polls effectively**, including choosing the right topics, optimizing poll structure, engaging your audience, analyzing results, and integrating polls into your broader content strategy.

1. Understanding the Power of Engagement with Polls

Polls are not just fun—they serve multiple purposes:

- **Encourage audience participation** – People love sharing opinions, especially when it's easy.

- **Gather feedback quickly** – Polls are a great way to get direct insights from your audience.

- **Boost visibility** – Engagement drives the X (Twitter) algorithm, increasing your reach.

- **Create interactive content** – A well-designed poll can spark discussions and debates.

To fully harness the power of polls, you need to design them with engagement in mind.

2. Choosing the Right Poll Topic

The first step in creating an engaging poll is selecting the right **topic**. It should be **relevant, timely, and interesting** to your audience. Here are some considerations:

Make It Relevant to Your Audience

Ask yourself:

- **What does my audience care about?**

- **What are common challenges or questions they face?**

- **What kind of discussions are trending in my niche?**

For example, if you run a **tech-focused account**, a poll like:
"Which smartphone feature matters most to you?"
[ ] Battery Life
[ ] Camera Quality
[ ] Screen Size
[ ] Performance

will likely get **higher engagement** than a generic poll about personal preferences.

Tap into Trending Topics

Polls related to **current events, industry trends, or viral discussions** are more likely to attract engagement.

Example:
"Will AI replace graphic designers in the next 10 years?"
[ ] Yes
[ ] No
[ ] Too soon to tell

By connecting your poll to trending discussions, you increase its likelihood of being discovered by a **broader audience**.

Keep It Simple and Clear

A poll should be **easy to understand at first glance**.

- Avoid complicated wording.

- Keep the question **short and to the point**.

- Limit the number of response options (2-4 choices is ideal).

Example of a **poorly structured** poll:
"What do you think about the advancements in machine learning algorithms and their application in autonomous vehicles?"

Better alternative:
"Are self-driving cars the future?"
[ ] Yes

[ ] No
[ ] Not sure

---

3. Optimizing Poll Structure

Even the best poll topic won't work if the structure isn't **optimized for engagement**. Consider the following:

The Ideal Number of Options

While X (Twitter) allows up to **four choices**, research suggests that engagement is **highest with 2-3 options**. Too many choices can overwhelm users and lead to lower participation.

- **2 options** – Best for "Yes/No" or binary questions.

- **3 options** – Allows a neutral or middle-ground option.

- **4 options** – Useful when asking for ranked preferences.

Example:
"What's your go-to drink in the morning?"
[ ] Coffee
[ ] Tea
[ ] Juice
[ ] Water

Using Emojis to Boost Engagement

Adding **emojis** can make your poll more **visually appealing and engaging**.

Example:
"How do you start your morning? ☀️🗔"
[☕] Coffee
[🍵] Tea
[🗔] Smoothie
[🗔] Water

Studies show that **tweets with emojis get more engagement**, so using them strategically can make a difference.

4. Timing Your Polls for Maximum Engagement

The timing of your poll plays a **huge role** in its success. Consider:

Posting During Peak Activity Hours

Different audiences are active at different times. Generally:

- **Morning (7-9 AM)** – Good for professional and productivity-related polls.
- **Lunch Break (12-2 PM)** – High engagement from casual users.
- **Evening (6-9 PM)** – Best for entertainment, opinions, and trending topics.
- **Weekend Polls** – Can perform well if they are fun or lighthearted.

If your audience is global, use **Twitter Analytics** to find when your followers are most active.

Aligning with Key Events or Holidays

If there's a big event happening, **tie your poll to it**.

Example:

- During the **World Cup**, a sports account could ask:
  "Who will win the World Cup this year?"
  [ ] Team A
  [ ] Team B

- Around **New Year's**, a lifestyle account might ask:
  "What's your #1 goal for the new year?"
  [ ] Fitness
  [ ] Career
  [ ] Relationships
  [ ] Travel

5. Encouraging Engagement Beyond the Poll

A poll should not be an **isolated post**—you need to encourage **further discussion**.

Adding a Follow-Up Question

Instead of just posting a poll, **add a follow-up tweet** to encourage replies.

Example:

"Which social media platform do you use most? (Poll below) 👆" Reply with **why** you picked your choice!

Retweeting and Engaging with Responses

- **Reply to comments** under your poll to keep the conversation going.

- **Retweet your own poll** with updates like:

    o "Wow! 500 votes already. Cast yours before it closes!"

    o "Surprising results so far—do you agree?"

Pinning Important Polls

If the poll is **important** (e.g., feedback for a product launch), pin it to the top of your profile for **maximum visibility**.

---

6. Analyzing Poll Results and Applying Insights

A poll is only useful if you learn from the results.

Tracking Participation Trends

Look at:

- **Total votes** – More votes indicate strong interest.

- **Reply engagement** – Are people commenting on the results?

- **Retweets and Shares** – Did the poll spark wider discussion?

Using Results to Create New Content

Example:

- If a poll reveals that **80% of people prefer Instagram over X (Twitter)**, you could write a **follow-up thread** discussing why.

- If a poll asks **"Do you want a guide on X monetization?"** and 70% say **yes**, you now have a content idea!

Conclusion

Polls are **powerful engagement tools** when used correctly. To maximize their impact:

✓ Choose **relevant, interesting topics**

✓ Keep poll questions **short and clear**

✓ Use **2-3 response options** for better engagement

✓ **Time polls strategically** to match audience activity

✓ **Encourage discussion** beyond the poll

✓ **Analyze results** to improve future content

By following these **best practices**, you can create polls that **engage your audience, spark discussions, and boost your reach** on X (Twitter).

CHAPTER IV
Growing Your Presence on X (Twitter)

5.1 Building a Personal or Business Brand

5.1.1 Crafting a Consistent Brand Voice

Introduction: The Importance of a Strong Brand Voice

In today's fast-paced digital landscape, having a consistent brand voice on X (Twitter) is essential for standing out. Whether you're building a personal brand as a thought leader or promoting a business, your brand voice defines how your audience perceives and engages with you. A strong and consistent brand voice helps establish credibility, fosters trust, and ensures your content resonates with your target audience.

This section will guide you through understanding what a brand voice is, how to develop one that aligns with your goals, and how to maintain consistency in your messaging.

What Is a Brand Voice?

A brand voice is the personality, tone, and style in which you communicate on X (Twitter). It reflects your values, mission, and the emotions you want to evoke in your audience. Your brand voice should be:

- **Authentic** – It should genuinely reflect your personality or company culture.

- **Consistent** – Your tone and messaging should remain the same across all posts.

- **Recognizable** – Your audience should instantly associate your tweets with your brand.

- **Engaging** – It should resonate with your audience and encourage interactions.

Think of your brand voice as the "personality" of your account. If your brand were a person, how would it speak? Would it be formal and professional, casual and friendly, or witty and humorous?

Step 1: Define Your Brand's Core Identity

Before crafting a brand voice, you need to define your brand's core identity. Ask yourself the following questions:

1. **What are your brand's core values?**

   o Example: Transparency, innovation, humor, professionalism, community-driven, etc.

2. **Who is your target audience?**

   o Example: Entrepreneurs, tech enthusiasts, students, corporate professionals, casual users, etc.

3. **How do you want your audience to feel when they engage with your content?**

   o Inspired, entertained, informed, reassured, motivated, etc.

4. **What adjectives best describe your brand?**

   o Example: Witty, authoritative, approachable, sophisticated, friendly, bold, etc.

Once you define your identity, use it as a foundation to shape your brand voice.

Step 2: Choose Your Brand's Tone and Style

Your tone and style determine how your brand voice is expressed in different contexts. Here are some common brand voice styles:

1. **Professional and Formal**

   o Ideal for corporate accounts, consultants, financial firms, or legal professionals.

- o Example:
  "Our latest report on industry trends is now available. Stay ahead with data-driven insights. #BusinessGrowth"

2. **Friendly and Approachable**

   - o Suitable for personal brands, customer service accounts, and lifestyle businesses.

   - o Example:
     "Hey everyone! We've got some exciting updates coming your way. Stay tuned! 🎉 #NewFeatures"

3. **Witty and Humorous**

   - o Works well for entertainment brands, media companies, and casual influencers.

   - o Example:
     "Mondays are rough. Coffee and memes are the only things keeping us alive. ☕😂 #MondayMood"

4. **Inspirational and Motivational**

   - o Ideal for coaches, authors, speakers, and fitness brands.

   - o Example:
     "Success isn't about luck; it's about consistency. Keep going, even on tough days. 💪 #MotivationMonday"

Your brand's tone should align with your target audience and industry while staying true to your identity.

Step 3: Establish Key Messaging Themes

Once you define your voice, create a list of key messaging themes that align with your brand. These themes should be recurring topics you consistently post about.

For example, if you are a **marketing consultant**, your key messaging themes could be:

- **Industry insights** – Sharing trends, reports, and expert opinions.

- **Actionable tips** – Providing marketing strategies that people can implement.

- **Personal experiences** – Sharing lessons learned from past projects.

- **Engagement-driven posts** – Asking questions, running polls, and encouraging discussions.

If you are a **tech startup**, your key messaging themes could be:

- **Product updates** – Announcing new features and improvements.

- **Customer success stories** – Showcasing how users benefit from your product.

- **Company culture** – Sharing behind-the-scenes content from your team.

- **Tech trends** – Discussing innovations and industry advancements.

By maintaining a set of key themes, your audience will know what to expect from your content, making your brand more recognizable.

Step 4: Maintain Consistency Across All Tweets

Consistency is the key to establishing a recognizable brand voice. Here's how you can ensure uniformity:

1. **Use a Consistent Writing Style**

   o Keep sentence structures, punctuation, and formatting uniform.

   o Decide on things like emoji usage, capitalization, and abbreviation preferences.

2. **Stick to a Regular Posting Schedule**

   o Frequent and predictable posting helps reinforce your brand voice.

   o Use scheduling tools like **X Pro (formerly TweetDeck)** to maintain consistency.

3. **Ensure Visual Consistency**

   o Use a consistent color scheme, fonts, and logo placement in images.

   o Stick to a unified aesthetic for all media (GIFs, videos, and infographics).

4. **Train Your Team (For Businesses and Brands)**

o   If multiple people manage your X (Twitter) account, provide a brand voice guideline.

o   Outline dos and don'ts to ensure everyone maintains a consistent tone.

Step 5: Adapt and Evolve Over Time

A brand voice isn't static—it evolves with time, audience preferences, and industry changes. Regularly assess:

1. **Engagement Metrics**

   o   Are your tweets receiving the expected likes, retweets, and replies?

   o   Do some types of content perform better than others?

2. **Audience Feedback**

   o   Are people responding positively to your tone?

   o   Do you need to adjust based on follower demographics and interests?

3. **Platform Trends**

   o   X (Twitter) frequently introduces new features (like Spaces, Communities, etc.).

   o   Adapt your voice to leverage emerging trends while staying true to your brand.

By analyzing performance and staying flexible, you can refine your brand voice to better connect with your audience.

Conclusion: Bringing It All Together

Crafting a consistent brand voice on X (Twitter) requires a clear understanding of your identity, tone, messaging themes, and audience engagement strategies. Whether you are an individual or a business, your voice should be authentic, engaging, and recognizable.

To recap:

✓ **Define your core identity** – Know your values, audience, and brand personality.

✓ **Choose a suitable tone and style** – Decide whether you want to be professional, casual, witty, or motivational.

✓ **Establish key messaging themes** – Maintain a content strategy that aligns with your expertise and brand mission.

✓ **Stay consistent** – Keep your tone, formatting, and posting schedule uniform.

✓ **Adapt over time** – Regularly analyze engagement and refine your approach.

By following these steps, you'll create a strong and memorable presence on X (Twitter), helping you build a loyal audience and achieve your personal or business branding goals.

5.1.2 Choosing the Right Content Strategy

Creating a strong content strategy is essential for building a successful presence on X (Twitter). Whether you're an individual looking to grow your personal brand or a business aiming to attract customers, having a clear, well-defined approach to content can make all the difference. In this section, we will explore how to choose the right content strategy by understanding your audience, defining your goals, leveraging different content types, and optimizing your approach for engagement and growth.

Understanding Your Audience

Before developing a content strategy, you must have a clear understanding of who your audience is. Your content should resonate with the people you want to reach, whether they are potential customers, industry professionals, or casual followers.

1. Identifying Your Target Audience

To create effective content, consider the following questions:

- Who are you trying to reach? (Demographics, interests, and behaviors)

- What problems do they have that your content can solve?

- What kind of content do they already engage with?

You can use **X (Twitter) Analytics** to gather insights into your audience's demographics, engagement patterns, and interests. Additionally, observing competitors and industry influencers can help you identify trends that appeal to your target audience.

2. Creating Audience Personas

Once you have data on your audience, create **personas**—fictional representations of your ideal followers. For example:

Persona 1: "Aspiring Entrepreneurs"

- Age: 25-35

- Interests: Business growth, productivity hacks, networking

- Challenges: Struggling to gain visibility and build credibility

- Preferred content: Business tips, success stories, motivational tweets

Persona 2: "Tech Enthusiasts"

- Age: 18-40

- Interests: Latest technology, AI, software development

- Challenges: Finding reliable sources of tech news

- Preferred content: Industry news, expert opinions, interactive discussions

By creating personas, you can tailor your content to meet the specific needs and interests of your audience.

Defining Your Content Goals

Your content strategy should align with your **overall objectives** on X (Twitter). Here are some common goals and the type of content that supports them:

Goal	Content Type
Increase brand awareness	Thought leadership posts, viral tweets, engaging polls
Drive website traffic	Blog post links, teaser content, call-to-action tweets
Boost engagement	Questions, interactive polls, Twitter Spaces discussions
Generate leads/sales	Product showcases, testimonials, promotional tweets
Establish authority	Educational threads, expert opinions, case studies

Clearly defining your goals helps you measure success and adjust your content accordingly.

Choosing the Right Content Formats

X (Twitter) offers various ways to share content. The most effective strategy involves **a mix of different content formats** to keep your audience engaged.

1. Single Tweets

Short, punchy tweets (up to 280 characters) are great for:

- Sharing quick insights

- Posting questions or prompts

- Making bold, attention-grabbing statements

Example:
"Struggling to get engagement on X? Here's a simple tip: Engage with others first. The more you give, the more you get. 🚀 #SocialMediaMarketing"

2. Threads (Tweetstorms)

Threads allow you to expand on a topic by linking multiple tweets together. They are perfect for:

- Explaining complex ideas

- Sharing personal experiences or case studies

- Breaking down step-by-step guides

Example:
"Want to increase engagement on X? Here's a 5-step framework that works 🧵"
(Thread continues with detailed steps)

3. Visual Content (Images, GIFs, Videos)

Posts with visuals tend to receive **higher engagement rates** than text-only tweets. You can use:

- Infographics to summarize key points

- GIFs to add humor and personality

- Short videos to explain concepts or showcase products

Example:
"Content is king, but engagement is the throne. Here's how to dominate X (Twitter) in 2024 📊🧵" (with an infographic attached)

4. Polls and Interactive Content

Polls encourage audience participation and are great for:

- Gathering opinions

- Driving engagement

- Understanding audience preferences

Example:
"What's your biggest challenge on X? ▢'
1▢▢ Growing followers
2▢▢ Increasing engagement
3▢▢ Creating content
4▢▢ Staying consistent

5. Twitter Spaces (Live Audio Conversations)

Hosting or joining **Twitter Spaces** can help you:

- Build credibility as a thought leader

- Engage with your community in real time

- Answer questions and provide insights

Example:
"Join me this Friday for a live Twitter Space on 'How to Build a Personal Brand on X' ▢▢ Ask me anything! #SocialMediaTips"

Creating a Consistent Posting Schedule

Consistency is key to maintaining visibility on X (Twitter). To keep your audience engaged, consider:

- **Posting Frequency:** Aim for 3-5 tweets per day, depending on your audience's activity.

- **Best Times to Post:** Use analytics to identify when your audience is most active.

- **Content Calendar:** Plan content in advance using scheduling tools like Buffer, Hootsuite, or X's native scheduling feature.

Example Posting Schedule

Day	Content Type	Example
Monday	Educational Thread	"How to create engaging content on X – A step-by-step guide □☝"
Tuesday	Interactive Poll	"Which social media platform do you use most?"
Wednesday	Visual Post	Infographic on content strategy
Thursday	Twitter Space Announcement	"Join us tomorrow for a live chat on personal branding!"
Friday	Engagement Tweet	"Drop your best marketing tip in the replies! ☝"

By following a structured schedule, you maintain consistency while keeping your content fresh and engaging.

Engaging with Your Audience

Your content strategy should not be one-sided. Engagement plays a crucial role in growing your presence. Here's how to make sure your content sparks conversations:

- **Reply to Comments:** Show appreciation for those who engage with your tweets.

- **Retweet and Quote-Tweet Others:** Share valuable content from other users while adding your insights.

- **Ask Questions:** Encourage followers to share their thoughts and experiences.

Example:
"What's the biggest lesson you've learned from using X (Twitter)? Drop your thoughts below! ☝"

Measuring and Optimizing Your Strategy

To refine your content strategy, track your performance using **X (Twitter) Analytics**. Key metrics to monitor include:

- **Engagement Rate:** Likes, replies, and retweets per post

- **Follower Growth:** Number of new followers over time

- **Impressions:** How many times your content is seen

- **Click-Through Rate (CTR):** How often users click your links

Based on these insights, adjust your strategy by:

- Doubling down on content that performs well

- Experimenting with new formats

- Posting at different times to test engagement

Conclusion

Choosing the right content strategy on X (Twitter) requires a balance of understanding your audience, selecting the right content formats, and maintaining consistency. By focusing on engagement, leveraging different content types, and optimizing based on data, you can build a strong and successful presence. Whether you're an individual or a business, a well-planned content strategy will help you grow your audience, establish authority, and achieve your goals on the platform.

Ready to take your content to the next level? In the next section, we'll explore how to grow your audience organically and attract the right followers!

5.2 Growing Your Audience Organically

5.2.1 How to Attract the Right Followers

Building an engaged audience on X (Twitter) is not just about accumulating numbers—it's about attracting the *right* followers. The right followers are those who are genuinely interested in your content, align with your brand or niche, and actively engage with your posts. Whether you're an individual looking to grow your personal influence or a business aiming to build brand awareness, cultivating a meaningful and relevant following requires a strategic approach.

This section will guide you through the best practices for attracting the right followers organically, without relying on paid promotions or bots. We'll cover the importance of defining your target audience, optimizing your profile, crafting engaging content, leveraging Twitter's features, and participating in meaningful conversations.

1. Define Your Target Audience

Before you can attract the right followers, you need to clearly define *who* your ideal audience is. Ask yourself:

- Who would benefit from my content?

- What topics do they care about?

- What problems do they have that I can help solve?

- What kind of content do they engage with the most?

For example, if you're a digital marketer, your target audience might be small business owners, aspiring marketers, and entrepreneurs looking for marketing tips. If you're a fitness coach, your audience could be people interested in health, exercise routines, and nutrition.

To refine your audience further, analyze other accounts in your niche. Look at the types of people who follow competitors or similar creators, and observe the kind of content that resonates with them.

Create a Follower Persona

A follower persona is a fictional representation of your ideal follower. It includes demographics (age, location, profession), interests, and behaviors. For instance:

- **Persona Name**: Entrepreneur Emma

- **Age**: 28-40

- **Interests**: Social media marketing, business growth, networking

- **Pain Points**: Struggles with brand visibility, engagement on X (Twitter)

- **Preferred Content**: Quick marketing tips, case studies, success stories

Having this persona in mind will help you tailor your content to attract the right followers.

2. Optimize Your X (Twitter) Profile for Maximum Appeal

Your profile is the first impression you make on potential followers. If your profile doesn't immediately communicate who you are and what value you offer, people are less likely to follow you.

Key Elements of an Optimized Profile

- **Username (@Handle)**: Make it simple, memorable, and relevant to your brand. Avoid excessive numbers or symbols.

- **Profile Picture**: Use a high-quality image. A professional headshot works best for personal brands, while businesses should use a recognizable logo.

- **Banner Image**: Your header image is prime real estate—use it to showcase your brand, slogan, or a call to action.

- **Bio**: Your bio should clearly state who you are, what you do, and why people should follow you. Use relevant keywords for discoverability. Example:

  - ✓ *Helping small businesses grow with smart marketing strategies | DM for consulting*

  - ✗ *Marketing expert | Love coffee | Tweeting random stuff*

- **Pinned Tweet**: Pin a high-value tweet at the top of your profile—this could be an introduction, a popular post, or a link to your website.

- **Link in Bio**: If you have a website, blog, or other relevant platform, include it in your profile.

3. Create Content That Attracts Followers

Attracting the right followers depends largely on the content you post. The goal is to create valuable, engaging, and shareable content that naturally draws people to your account.

Content Types That Attract Followers

1. **Educational Content** – Teach something valuable (e.g., "5 tips to improve your X (Twitter) engagement").

2. **Inspirational Content** – Share success stories, quotes, or lessons learned.

3. **Entertaining Content** – Use humor, memes, or lighthearted commentary to engage followers.

4. **Engagement-Driven Content** – Ask questions, run polls, or start discussions.

5. **Behind-the-Scenes Content** – Show the personal side of your brand to build authenticity.

Tweet Formats That Work Well

- **Threads** – Long-form content broken into a series of connected tweets. Great for storytelling and deep dives.

- **Polls** – Interactive and engaging. Example: *"What's the biggest challenge you face in social media marketing?"*

- **Videos & GIFs** – Visual content tends to get higher engagement than plain text.

- **Lists & Tips** – Quick, actionable advice performs well. Example: *"3 simple ways to improve your content strategy:"*

Be Consistent

Posting consistently increases your visibility. Aim for **at least 3-5 tweets per day**, including a mix of different content types.

4. Leverage Twitter Features to Expand Your Reach

Use Hashtags Wisely

Hashtags help categorize your tweets and make them discoverable by people interested in your niche.

- ✓ Use **2-3 relevant hashtags** per tweet.
- ✓ Research trending and industry-specific hashtags.
- ✗ Avoid overloading your tweets with too many hashtags.

Engage with Trending Topics

Participate in trending conversations to increase visibility. Ensure your contributions are meaningful and aligned with your brand.

Tag and Mention Others

When sharing valuable content, tag relevant people (without spamming). This can lead to more engagement and potential retweets.

Utilize X (Twitter) Spaces

Hosting or participating in live audio conversations on Spaces helps you connect with new followers who are interested in your niche.

5. Engage with Your Audience to Build Relationships

Growing a loyal following isn't just about pushing content—it's about engaging with others.

Best Practices for Engagement

- **Reply to Comments** – Show appreciation for those who interact with your tweets.
- **Engage with Other Creators** – Commenting on and retweeting relevant content increases your visibility.
- **Ask Questions** – Encourage conversation by prompting followers to share their thoughts.
- **Run Giveaways or Contests** – These can attract followers if done strategically.

6. Track Your Growth and Adjust Your Strategy

Monitor Analytics

Use Twitter Analytics to track which types of tweets perform best, when your audience is most active, and how your engagement rates evolve.

Test and Iterate

Experiment with different content formats, posting times, and engagement strategies to see what works best for your audience.

Conclusion

Attracting the right followers on X (Twitter) requires a mix of strategy, consistency, and engagement. By defining your target audience, optimizing your profile, posting valuable content, leveraging platform features, and actively engaging with others, you can build an authentic and engaged following.

Growing organically takes time, but focusing on quality over quantity ensures that you attract followers who genuinely care about your content and are more likely to support your long-term goals.

Now that you know how to attract the right followers, let's move on to the next section: **"Engaging with Influencers and Thought Leaders"**, where we'll explore how collaborations can further boost your presence on X (Twitter).

5.2.2 Engaging with Influencers and Thought Leaders

Engaging with influencers and thought leaders on X (Twitter) is one of the most effective ways to grow your audience organically. These individuals already have a strong following, and by interacting with them strategically, you can increase your visibility, gain credibility, and attract the right audience to your profile.

In this section, we'll explore the importance of engaging with influencers and thought leaders, how to identify the right people to interact with, and specific strategies you can use to build meaningful relationships.

Understanding the Role of Influencers and Thought Leaders

Who Are Influencers and Thought Leaders?

- **Influencers**: These are individuals who have a large following and can influence public opinion, trends, or purchasing decisions within a specific niche. They may be celebrities, industry experts, or content creators who have built a strong brand presence.

- **Thought Leaders**: Unlike influencers, thought leaders are recognized for their expertise, insights, and innovative ideas in a particular industry. They often contribute to discussions, share valuable knowledge, and set trends rather than simply following them.

Both influencers and thought leaders hold significant sway over their audience, making them valuable allies in expanding your reach on X (Twitter).

Why Engaging with Influencers and Thought Leaders Matters

1. **Increased Visibility** – When you engage with influencers, their followers are more likely to notice and interact with your content.

2. **Credibility Boost** – If a trusted expert in your niche acknowledges you, your credibility and authority improve.

3. **Networking Opportunities** – Building relationships with these individuals can lead to collaborations, partnerships, or speaking opportunities.

4. **More Organic Growth** – Instead of relying on paid ads, engaging with industry leaders helps you attract followers who are genuinely interested in your content.

How to Identify the Right Influencers and Thought Leaders

Not every influencer or thought leader is the right fit for your brand. You need to be strategic about whom you engage with.

Finding Relevant Influencers in Your Niche

1. **Use X (Twitter) Search and Hashtags** – Search for keywords and hashtags related to your industry. See who is frequently mentioned and has high engagement.

2. **Follow Industry Conversations** – Pay attention to the people who are driving conversations in your field.

3. **Use Influencer Discovery Tools** – Platforms like Followerwonk, BuzzSumo, and HypeAuditor can help you find relevant influencers based on engagement, reach, and niche.

4. **Check Engagement Levels** – Look beyond follower count. Engagement rate (likes, retweets, replies) is a more accurate measure of influence.

Assessing Thought Leaders

- Look for professionals who frequently share valuable insights, research, or commentary in your industry.

- Check if they are featured in industry articles, podcasts, or conference panels.

- Observe the quality of their interactions—do they engage in meaningful discussions, or do they just broadcast their content?

Strategies for Engaging with Influencers and Thought Leaders

Once you have identified the right influencers and thought leaders, the next step is to engage with them in a way that is both natural and valuable.

1. Follow and Observe First

Before jumping into conversations, take some time to observe how an influencer interacts with their audience. What topics do they frequently discuss? What style of communication do they use? Understanding their approach will help you engage more effectively.

2. Engage with Their Content Regularly

- **Like and Retweet Their Posts** – Show appreciation for their insights by liking and retweeting their content.

- **Add Thoughtful Comments** – Instead of generic replies like "Great post!", add meaningful input that contributes to the conversation. Example:

Influencer: "AI is transforming the future of marketing!"
Your response: "Absolutely! AI-driven personalization is reshaping customer engagement. Have you seen the latest study from MIT on this?"

- **Ask Questions** – Engage them in discussions by asking insightful questions that invite a response.

3. Share Their Content and Tag Them

- If an influencer writes an article or shares an important update, share it with your audience and tag them.

- Add your thoughts to the post to show that you are genuinely interested in their content. Example:

"Really insightful take from @InfluencerName on the future of remote work! This aligns with what we've been seeing in our research. What do you all think?"

4. Participate in Their Conversations

- Join Twitter Spaces hosted by influencers and contribute to discussions.

- If they start a poll or thread, engage with it and offer your perspective.

- If they reply to someone else's post, join the conversation naturally.

5. Create Content That Attracts Their Attention

- Post insights or data that align with an influencer's interests and tag them if relevant.

- Mention them in "Top X Influencers in [Industry]" lists.

- Write a Twitter thread on a topic they have recently discussed and reference their insights.

6. Offer Value Before Asking for Anything

Influencers receive countless messages asking for retweets or collaborations. Instead of immediately requesting something, focus on giving value.

- Share insights that complement their content.

- Introduce them to relevant contacts.

- Offer a different perspective or additional data on a topic they care about.

7. Collaborate on Content

Once you've built a rapport, explore collaboration opportunities:

- **Co-host a Twitter Space** – Invite them to discuss a topic in a live audio conversation.

- **Guest Post or Interview** – Offer to feature them in an article or podcast.

- **Joint Threads** – Engage in a Twitter thread where you and the influencer contribute insights on a shared topic.

Common Mistakes to Avoid

1. Over-Promoting Yourself

Don't constantly reply to influencers with links to your content. Focus on genuine engagement.

2. Being Too Aggressive

If you tag an influencer too often or spam their posts, you might come across as desperate or annoying.

3. Expecting Immediate Results

Building relationships takes time. Don't expect influencers to notice you after one interaction. Stay consistent.

4. Not Adding Value

If your comments and replies don't contribute to the discussion, influencers will be less likely to engage with you.

Final Thoughts

Engaging with influencers and thought leaders on X (Twitter) is one of the most powerful organic growth strategies available. By building genuine connections, providing value, and participating in meaningful conversations, you can increase your visibility, attract the right followers, and establish yourself as a credible voice in your niche.

Start by identifying the right people to engage with, consistently interact with their content, and explore collaboration opportunities when the time is right. Over time, this approach will help you grow a strong and engaged audience on X (Twitter).

5.3 Content Strategies for Engagement

5.3.1 Using Visuals: GIFs, Images, and Videos

Visual content has become a powerful tool on X (Twitter), significantly enhancing engagement, increasing shareability, and helping users stand out in an ever-crowded digital space. While X (Twitter) was initially text-based, it has evolved into a platform where multimedia elements such as **GIFs, images, and videos** play a crucial role in capturing attention. In this section, we will explore why visual content is important, how to use each type effectively, and best practices for maximizing engagement with GIFs, images, and videos.

The Power of Visual Content on X (Twitter)

Research consistently shows that tweets with **visual elements receive higher engagement rates** than text-only tweets. Here are some compelling statistics and reasons why using visuals can improve your performance on X (Twitter):

- **Tweets with images receive 150% more retweets** than those without.

- **Videos are six times more likely to be retweeted** compared to text-based tweets.

- **GIFs increase engagement by up to 55%**, making them an effective way to add personality and humor to your posts.

The primary reasons why visual content performs well include:

- **Attention-Grabbing**: People naturally focus on images and videos over plain text.

- **Easier Comprehension**: A well-designed image or video can convey a message faster than words alone.

- **Emotional Connection**: Visuals evoke emotions, making content more relatable and memorable.

- **Better Storytelling**: A compelling image or video can tell a story more effectively than a long block of text.

Now, let's dive into how you can use GIFs, images, and videos strategically on X (Twitter).

Using GIFs to Enhance Engagement

What Are GIFs and Why Use Them?

GIFs (Graphics Interchange Format) are short, looping animations that add movement and humor to posts. They are widely used on X (Twitter) to express emotions, reactions, or provide quick snippets of information.

Best Practices for Using GIFs

1. **Use GIFs to Enhance Emotions**

   o   GIFs can express humor, excitement, frustration, or enthusiasm better than text alone.

   o   Example: Instead of saying "I'm so excited for this!" you can add a GIF of someone cheering or celebrating.

2. **React to Trends and Conversations**

   o   GIFs are great for participating in trending topics, memes, and viral conversations.

   o   Example: If a major event is happening, use a relevant GIF to join the discussion.

3. **Make Your Tweets More Playful**

   o   Adding a GIF to a reply can make your response more engaging and fun.

   o   Example: Instead of a simple "Thank you!", adding a GIF of someone saying "Thanks a lot!" can feel more expressive.

4. **Use GIFs in Polls and Questions**

   o   If you're asking a question, a GIF can make it more engaging.

   o   Example: If you're polling your audience about their favorite coffee type, adding a GIF of a steaming coffee cup can increase interaction.

5. **Keep It Relevant**

   o   While GIFs are fun, they should match the tone and message of your tweet. Avoid using random GIFs that do not relate to your content.

Where to Find and Create GIFs

- **X (Twitter) has a built-in GIF library** powered by Giphy and Tenor. You can simply click the GIF button when composing a tweet.

- **You can create custom GIFs** using tools like **Giphy, EZGIF, or Canva**. These allow you to make branded or unique animations tailored to your content.

Using Images to Capture Attention

Why Images Matter on X (Twitter)

Images make your tweets visually appealing, help break up text, and allow for more creative expression. A single image can **convey complex ideas quickly** and make your tweets more shareable.

Types of Images You Can Use

1. **Infographics**

   - Great for sharing data, statistics, and educational content.

   - Example: A startup founder can post an infographic showing their company's growth over the years.

2. **Branded Graphics**

   - Images with company logos, colors, and branding elements can strengthen brand identity.

   - Example: A business can share a promotional tweet with a visually appealing branded image.

3. **Screenshots**

   - Useful for tutorials, how-to guides, or showcasing conversations.

   - Example: A tech influencer might share a screenshot explaining a new software update.

4. **Memes and Relatable Images**

   - Adding humor through memes can increase shareability.

    o Example: A marketing expert might share a meme about "client feedback" to engage their audience.

5. **Behind-the-Scenes (BTS) Photos**

    o Giving your followers a glimpse of your personal or professional life builds authenticity.

    o Example: A musician might post a BTS image from a studio recording session.

Best Practices for Using Images on X (Twitter)

1. **Use High-Quality, Clear Images**

    o Blurry or pixelated images can make your tweets look unprofessional. Always ensure high resolution.

2. **Add Text to Images When Necessary**

    o Overlaying text on an image can help reinforce your message. However, keep it readable.

3. **Make Images Mobile-Friendly**

    o Since most users browse X (Twitter) on their phones, ensure images are optimized for mobile screens.

4. **Use the Right Image Dimensions**

    o The ideal size for shared images is **1600 x 900 pixels**, while profile banners should be **1500 x 500 pixels**.

Using Videos to Increase Engagement

Why Videos Are Powerful on X (Twitter)

Video content is one of the most effective ways to engage audiences, deliver messages quickly, and even go viral. With X (Twitter) prioritizing video content in its algorithm, **tweets with videos get 10x more engagement than text-only tweets**.

Types of Videos to Use on X (Twitter)

1. **Short-Form Videos (Under 60 Seconds)**

- o   Quick, engaging, and perfect for storytelling.
- o   Example: A chef might post a **30-second recipe tutorial**.

2. **Explainer or How-To Videos**

- o   Great for sharing knowledge and expertise.
- o   Example: A fitness coach could post a **short workout demonstration**.

3. **Live Videos (X Spaces with Video)**

- o   Broadcasting live lets you connect with your audience in real time.

4. **Customer Testimonials or Product Demos**

- o   Businesses can use these to build credibility.

Best Practices for Using Videos on X (Twitter)

1. **Keep Videos Short and Engaging** (15–60 seconds works best)

2. **Include Captions** for accessibility and users who scroll without sound.

3. **Start Strong** – The first **3 seconds are crucial** to capture attention.

4. **Use a Clear Call-to-Action (CTA)** – Encourage users to like, comment, or share.

Conclusion

Using **GIFs, images, and videos** effectively on X (Twitter) can **boost engagement, increase visibility, and make your content more memorable**. By incorporating the right visuals in your tweets, you can capture audience attention, improve storytelling, and grow your presence on the platform.

Creating Custom Visuals for X (Twitter)

Custom visuals are a fantastic way to set your brand apart, making your tweets stand out in a crowded feed. By creating images, GIFs, and videos that are tailored to your audience and message, you can increase both engagement and brand recognition. Let's go over the key steps and tools involved in creating impactful custom visuals for X (Twitter).

1. Why Custom Visuals Matter

Custom visuals help you create a unique identity on X (Twitter). Here's why they are so important:

- **Brand Identity**: Custom images help reinforce your brand's visual identity (logo, color scheme, fonts).

- **Differentiation**: Customized visuals are less likely to blend into the noise of generic stock photos.

- **Higher Engagement**: Tweets with unique images or videos are more likely to be shared and retweeted.

2. Types of Custom Visuals You Can Create

a) Branded Images

Branded images combine your logo, company colors, and typography with visuals that align with your message. They can be used to:

- Promote products, services, or events.

- Share announcements or important information.

- Tell your brand's story with imagery that matches your voice.

How to Create Branded Images:

- **Tools**: Canva, Adobe Spark, and PicMonkey are popular tools for creating branded graphics.

- **Tip**: Start with a template that fits the platform's dimensions (1600x900 pixels for images). Customize the template with your brand's colors, fonts, and logo.

b) Infographics

Infographics are a powerful way to share data, facts, and statistics in a visual format. They allow followers to digest complex information quickly.

How to Create Infographics:

- **Tools**: Canva, Piktochart, and Venngage. These platforms provide pre-built templates for infographics.

- **Tip**: Stick to a simple design—avoid overwhelming your audience with too much text or data. Highlight key points using bold colors or icons.

c) Custom GIFs

Custom GIFs are a fun way to engage your audience. They add movement to your tweets and can easily be shared, helping to boost your visibility.

How to Create Custom GIFs:

- **Tools**: Giphy's GIF maker, EZGIF, or Canva (which now supports GIF creation).

- **Tip**: Use GIFs that are relevant to your tweet's context, whether it's humor, emotion, or a reaction. Keep them under 5-10 seconds to ensure they loop smoothly.

d) Branded Videos

Videos are an excellent way to increase engagement, and custom videos can further amplify your brand's message.

How to Create Branded Videos:

- **Tools**: Adobe Premiere Rush, Final Cut Pro, and Canva Video Editor. These tools help you edit videos with transitions, text overlays, and other visual effects.

- **Tip**: Keep your videos short (under 60 seconds) to maintain viewer interest. Always include a CTA (Call to Action) at the end.

3. Tips for Designing Effective Custom Visuals

- **Consistency is Key**: Ensure that your visuals align with your brand's visual identity. Stick to a consistent color palette, typography, and style across all graphics.

- **Simplicity Over Clutter**: Avoid overcrowding your visuals with too much text or too many elements. Focus on one message per graphic.

- **Incorporate CTA**: If your goal is to drive action (e.g., click, sign-up, purchase), always include a call-to-action (CTA) in your visuals.

- **Make It Mobile-Friendly**: Since most users browse X (Twitter) on mobile devices, ensure your visuals are optimized for small screens.

Using Analytics to Measure Engagement on X (Twitter)

Once you start posting custom visuals and creating engaging content, it's crucial to track and measure how your audience responds. Analytics provide valuable insights into what's working, what isn't, and how you can optimize your content strategy. Here's how you can use analytics to measure engagement effectively.

1. Key Metrics to Track on X (Twitter)

To determine the effectiveness of your posts, you should track the following engagement metrics:

- **Engagement Rate**: The percentage of people who interacted with your tweet compared to the total number of impressions.

- **Impressions**: The number of times your tweet was seen.

- **Retweets and Shares**: The number of times your tweet was shared by others, indicating high engagement.

- **Likes**: The number of likes shows how well your audience connects with your content.

- **Replies**: Tracking the number of replies can help you gauge how much conversation your tweet has generated.

- **Clicks**: This includes any clicks on links in your tweets, such as links to your website, blog, or product page.

2. Using Twitter Analytics

Twitter provides an in-built analytics tool that can give you a comprehensive view of your account's performance. Here's how you can use it effectively:

- **How to Access**: Go to analytics.twitter.com and log in with your account.

- **Dashboard Overview**: Twitter Analytics will show you a 28-day summary of your account's performance, including impressions, engagement rate, top tweets, and more.

Key Insights from Twitter Analytics:

- **Top Tweets**: This section shows the tweets with the most engagement over the past month, helping you understand what content your followers prefer.

- **Audience Insights**: Twitter Analytics provides information on your audience's demographics, such as location, gender, interests, and more. This can help you tailor your content to better suit your audience.

- **Engagement Metrics**: Track metrics like engagement rate, impressions, and clicks to gauge how well your visuals are performing.

3. Third-Party Analytics Tools

For more in-depth analysis, you can use third-party tools like **Sprout Social, Hootsuite, Buffer**, or **SocialBee**. These platforms allow you to track multiple accounts, schedule content, and get detailed insights into your audience's behavior.

How to Use Third-Party Tools:

- **Social Listening**: Track mentions of your brand or keywords across the platform to see what people are saying.

- **Content Performance**: Monitor the performance of all your posts across different time frames and campaigns.

- **Optimize Posting Times**: Many tools also provide insights into the best times to post based on your audience's activity, allowing you to schedule tweets for maximum reach.

4. Iterating and Optimizing Your Visual Content

Analytics not only helps you track engagement but also provides insight into what works and what doesn't. Here's how you can use this data to optimize your content:

- **Identify Top Performers**: Look at your most successful posts—what kind of visuals did you use? What topics were covered? Replicate these successful elements in future posts.

- **Test Different Visual Formats**: Use A/B testing (posting different types of visuals or messaging) to compare performance.

- **Refine Your Strategy**: If certain types of visuals (e.g., videos or infographics) are getting more engagement, increase their frequency in your content strategy.

Conclusion

Creating custom visuals is a key strategy for standing out on X (Twitter). By using **GIFs, images, and videos**, you can engage your audience in ways that text alone cannot. With tools like Canva, Adobe Spark, and Giphy, it's easier than ever to create professional, branded content that drives engagement.

In addition, tracking **engagement analytics** helps you understand how well your content is performing and informs future strategy decisions. By using insights from Twitter Analytics and third-party tools, you can refine your approach, test new formats, and optimize your visuals for maximum impact.

5.3.2 Creating High-Quality and Shareable Content

Creating high-quality and shareable content on X (formerly Twitter) is essential for building engagement, growing your audience, and establishing credibility. The platform thrives on fast-paced conversations, trending topics, and real-time interactions, making it crucial to craft content that resonates with users while encouraging them to engage, share, and amplify your message.

In this section, we will explore the key principles of high-quality content, strategies for maximizing shareability, the role of storytelling, and tips for formatting posts effectively.

1. Understanding What Makes Content High-Quality

Before diving into tactics for creating shareable content, it's essential to understand what makes content high-quality. On X, high-quality content typically meets the following criteria:

- **Valuable:** It provides useful information, insights, or entertainment.

- **Engaging:** It encourages interaction through likes, retweets, replies, and discussions.

- **Concise:** Since X has a character limit, the message must be clear and direct.

- **Authentic:** Users value genuine and relatable posts over overly polished or robotic content.

- **Visually Appealing:** Posts with images, videos, or GIFs tend to perform better than plain text.

2. Strategies for Creating Shareable Content

Leveraging Trending Topics and Hashtags

One of the most effective ways to increase shareability is by participating in trending conversations. X has a **Trending** section where users can see popular topics at any given moment.

- **Use Trending Hashtags:** Find relevant trending hashtags and incorporate them into your posts. However, ensure they align with your brand or message rather than forcing irrelevant trends.

- **Timely Reactions:** Reacting to breaking news, viral trends, or cultural moments can boost engagement and visibility.

- **Leverage X Polls and Questions:** Encourage interaction by asking questions related to trending topics.

💡 *Example:*
If #AIRevolution is trending, a tech influencer might tweet:
"How do you think AI will impact job markets in the next five years? #AIRevolution"

Writing Tweets That Encourage Engagement

To create content that people want to share, focus on structuring your tweets for maximum engagement. Some effective tweet structures include:

Lists and How-To Tweets

People love bite-sized, actionable advice. Formatting tweets as quick lists or step-by-step guides makes them highly shareable.

💡 *Example:*
🚀 **5 Tips for Writing Viral Tweets** 🚀
1️⃣ Use a strong hook
2️⃣ Keep it concise

3️⃣Add value (educate or entertain)
4️⃣Use visuals (GIFs, images)
5️⃣Engage with replies
#TwitterTips #ContentMarketing

Thought-Provoking or Relatable Statements

Relatable and opinion-driven tweets often get high engagement because people resonate with them.

💡 *Example:*
"The best way to grow on X? Stop obsessing over followers and start focusing on VALUE."

Open-Ended Questions

Encouraging users to respond increases engagement and visibility.

💡 *Example:*
"What's the best piece of career advice you've ever received? Drop it below! ⬇️ "

The Power of Storytelling

People connect with stories more than with plain facts or promotions. Using storytelling in tweets can significantly increase their shareability.

Personal Anecdotes

Sharing personal experiences makes tweets more relatable.

💡 *Example:*
"Five years ago, I was struggling to get 100 followers. Today, I have 100,000. Here's what changed..."

Success Stories and Lessons Learned

People love motivational content and success stories.

💡 *Example:*
"I got my first client from a single tweet. Want to know how? Read on..."

Using a Thread for Longer Stories

X allows users to create **Threads**, where multiple tweets are connected in a sequence. Threads are great for storytelling, sharing deep insights, or providing tutorials.

💡 *Example:*
"🚀 How I built a $10,000/month business on X (without paid ads). A thread 🧵"

Using Visuals to Boost Engagement

Posts with **images, GIFs, videos, and infographics** get significantly more engagement than plain text tweets.

Adding Eye-Catching Images

Images should be **high-quality, relevant, and optimized** for mobile viewing.

💡 *Example:*
A productivity expert tweeting about focus techniques could attach a **simple infographic** summarizing key points.

Leveraging GIFs for Humor and Engagement

GIFs can make posts feel **more relatable and fun**.

💡 *Example:*
"When I see my tweet getting thousands of likes overnight:"
Insert GIF of someone celebrating 🎉

Short-Form Videos

Videos under **30-60 seconds** perform well on X. Use them for quick tutorials, behind-the-scenes content, or mini-vlogs.

Structuring Your Tweets for Maximum Readability

Even if your content is great, poor formatting can reduce its impact. Here's how to make your tweets more readable:

- **Use Line Breaks:** Avoid long paragraphs; space out text for easier reading.

- **Use Emojis (But Don't Overdo It):** Emojis make tweets more visually appealing and expressive.

- **Keep It Concise:** Stick to 1-2 sentences when possible.

💡 *Example:*

🚀 **Want to boost engagement on X?**

Here's what you need to do:

✓ Use strong hooks

✓ Add value (educate or entertain)

✓ Post at peak hours

✓ Engage with replies

3. Analyzing What Works and Improving Over Time

Even the best content creators need to **analyze their performance and adjust** their strategies.

Using X Analytics

X provides **analytics** that help you track:

- Engagement (likes, retweets, replies)

- Impressions (how many people saw your tweet)

- Click-through rate (if you shared a link)

A/B Testing Different Content Types

Experiment with different types of tweets and track what works best:

- Do text-only tweets perform better than image-based tweets?

- Do question-based tweets get more replies than statement-based tweets?

- Does posting at a specific time lead to better engagement?

4. Common Mistakes to Avoid

Even experienced users make mistakes that limit their engagement. Here are some to watch out for:

Posting Without a Strategy

Randomly tweeting without understanding your audience reduces your chances of getting engagement.

Over-Promotion Without Value

If every tweet is a sales pitch, followers may lose interest. Aim for an **80/20 balance** between value-driven content and promotions.

Ignoring Replies and Engagement

If someone engages with your tweet, reply! Conversations help boost visibility.

Conclusion

Creating high-quality and shareable content on X requires a mix of **clarity, engagement, visuals, storytelling, and strategic posting**. By understanding what makes content compelling, leveraging trending topics, using the right formats, and continuously analyzing performance, you can significantly increase your reach and build a strong presence on the platform.

5.3.3 The Best Times to Post

One of the most crucial aspects of maximizing engagement on X (Twitter) is timing. Posting at the right times can significantly increase the visibility of your tweets, helping you reach a wider audience, gain more interactions, and grow your influence on the platform. However, the "best time" to post isn't a one-size-fits-all answer—it depends on your audience, location, industry, and content type.

In this section, we'll explore how X's algorithm influences post visibility, general recommendations for posting times, industry-specific best times, tools to analyze audience activity, and how to experiment and optimize your posting schedule.

---

1. How X (Twitter)'s Algorithm Affects Visibility

Before diving into the best times to post, it's important to understand how X's algorithm impacts what users see. Unlike a strict chronological timeline, X uses an algorithm to determine which tweets appear on a user's feed. Key factors influencing visibility include:

- **Recency** – Newer tweets are more likely to appear in the feed, especially for users who have their timeline set to "Latest Tweets."

- **Engagement** – Tweets with more likes, comments, retweets, and quote tweets are prioritized.

- **User Preferences** – If a user frequently interacts with your content, your tweets are more likely to appear in their feed.

- **Relevance** – X promotes content that aligns with trending topics and popular discussions.

Understanding these factors helps you realize why posting at peak engagement times is critical—more people will see your content when they are online and active, increasing the likelihood of interactions.

2. General Best Times to Post on X (Twitter)

Although the ideal posting time varies, research from various social media analytics companies suggests general guidelines:

Best Days to Post:

- **Midweek (Tuesday to Thursday)** tends to be the most active time for engagement.

- **Mondays** are slower as people catch up on work, while **Fridays** show some decline as people transition into the weekend.

- **Weekends** can work well for certain industries but generally have lower engagement.

Best Times to Post:

- **Early Morning (7:00 AM – 9:00 AM)** – People check their phones as they wake up or during their commute.

- **Midday (12:00 PM – 1:00 PM)** – Lunchtime breaks often lead to increased social media activity.

- **Late Afternoon (3:00 PM – 6:00 PM)** – Users check X during their afternoon break or while finishing work.

- **Evening (7:00 PM – 10:00 PM)** – Engagement spikes as people relax and browse social media before bed.

Worst Times to Post:

- **Late at Night (11:00 PM – 5:00 AM)** – Activity drops significantly, unless you target a global audience in different time zones.

- **Weekend Mornings (Before 9:00 AM)** – Engagement is often low as people sleep in or spend time offline.

3. Industry-Specific Best Times to Post

Different industries have different peak engagement periods. If you are running a personal brand or business, consider these industry-specific insights:

- **Tech & Startups** – Peak engagement happens **Tuesday to Thursday between 9:00 AM and 12:00 PM** when professionals check updates.

- **Entertainment & Media** – Best times are **evenings and weekends** when people unwind and consume content.

- **E-commerce & Retail** – Posting during **lunch breaks and evenings** works best, as people browse shopping options during free time.

- **Finance & Business** – Peak hours are **before and after traditional work hours (7:00 AM – 9:00 AM and 5:00 PM – 7:00 PM)** as professionals stay updated on market trends.

- **Health & Wellness** – Engagement is highest in the **early mornings and late evenings**, when people focus on self-care.

- **Education & Learning** – Best engagement occurs **midweek (Tuesday – Thursday) between 12:00 PM and 4:00 PM** as students and educators take breaks.

Understanding these trends helps you align your posting schedule with when your audience is most active.

4. How to Find Your Audience's Best Time to Post

While general recommendations are useful, your specific audience may have unique behavior patterns. To determine when *your* followers are most active, use the following strategies:

1. Analyze Your X (Twitter) Analytics

- Navigate to **X Analytics** (analytics.twitter.com) to track post performance.
- Check the **Engagement Rate** to identify when your tweets get the most interactions.
- Look at **Follower Activity** to see when your audience is online.

2. Use Third-Party Tools

Several tools help analyze your best posting times, including:

- **TweetDeck** – Helps monitor engagement trends in real time.
- **Hootsuite & Buffer** – Provide recommendations for optimal posting schedules.
- **Sprout Social & SocialPilot** – Offer AI-driven insights on when to post.

3. Experiment with Different Posting Times

- Test posting at different times throughout the day and track engagement.
- Identify trends over a few weeks to determine peak audience activity.
- Consider **A/B testing** (posting similar content at different times) to compare performance.

5. Optimizing Your Posting Schedule for Maximum Engagement

Once you identify the best times to post, optimize your strategy using these best practices:

1. Post Consistently

- Posting regularly increases visibility and keeps your audience engaged.
- Aim for **1–3 tweets per day** for optimal reach.

2. Schedule Tweets in Advance

- Use scheduling tools like **TweetDeck, Buffer, or Hootsuite** to maintain consistency.

- Plan tweets based on your best engagement times.

3. Leverage Peak and Off-Peak Hours

- Post **high-value content (threads, major announcements, promotions) during peak hours**.

- Use **off-peak hours for experimental content** (polls, casual tweets, behind-the-scenes updates).

4. Engage in Real Time

- Be active when your audience is online—respond to replies, retweet, and engage with trending topics.

- If posting at non-work hours, use scheduling tools but also check notifications periodically to interact.

5. Consider Global Time Zones

- If your audience is international, schedule tweets to cover different time zones.

- Use insights from analytics to identify key geographic locations.

6. Key Takeaways and Final Thoughts

- **Timing matters**, but it's not the only factor—high-quality content is still crucial.

- **General best posting times** are **early morning, midday, late afternoon, and evening** on **Tuesdays to Thursdays**.

- **Industry-specific trends** can influence when your audience is most active.

- **X Analytics and third-party tools** help identify the best times based on your audience.

- **Experiment and optimize** to find what works best for your unique following.

By understanding and leveraging the best times to post, you can significantly enhance engagement, grow your audience, and maximize your impact on X (Twitter).

5.4 Dealing with Trolls and Negative Comments

5.4.1 How to Handle Online Criticism

Social media platforms like X (formerly Twitter) provide a powerful space for individuals and businesses to share their thoughts, connect with audiences, and build their personal or professional brands. However, along with the benefits of increased visibility comes the inevitable challenge of online criticism. Whether it's constructive feedback, harsh criticism, or outright trolling, learning how to handle negative comments effectively is crucial for maintaining your credibility and mental well-being.

In this section, we will explore how to distinguish between constructive criticism and trolling, the best strategies for responding to criticism, and how to protect yourself from unnecessary negativity while continuing to grow on the platform.

1. Understanding Different Types of Criticism

Before reacting to a negative comment, it's important to understand the intent behind it. Not all criticism is harmful—some can be valuable and help you improve. Here are the main types of criticism you may encounter on X:

a. Constructive Criticism

Constructive criticism is meant to provide helpful feedback and suggestions for improvement. It is usually polite and well-intended. For example:

- *"I liked your thread, but I think you could add more sources to support your arguments."*

- *"Your latest post was insightful, but I disagree with your conclusion. Here's why..."*

Even though it may not always be pleasant to hear, constructive criticism should be welcomed as an opportunity for growth.

b. Harsh but Honest Feedback

Sometimes, people express their opinions bluntly without intending to be rude. These comments may seem aggressive, but they can still contain valuable insights. For example:

- *"This take is completely wrong. Do some research before posting."*

- *"Your post is misleading. Here's the correct information..."*

Instead of reacting emotionally, consider whether there is any truth to the criticism and if you can use it to improve your content.

c. Malicious Criticism and Trolling

Some users leave negative comments simply to provoke a reaction. These comments are often personal attacks, unfounded accusations, or offensive statements. Examples include:

- *"You're an idiot. Stop posting nonsense."*

- *"Your content is trash, and so are you."*

These comments are not meant to help you improve but rather to cause distress. Learning to ignore or block such interactions is essential.

---

2. Best Practices for Responding to Criticism

How you respond to criticism on X can shape how others perceive you. Here are some strategies for handling different types of criticism effectively.

a. Take a Moment Before Responding

It's easy to react emotionally to negative comments, especially if they feel unfair. However, before responding, take a moment to assess the situation. Ask yourself:

- Is this comment worth responding to?

- Does the person have a valid point?

- Will engaging in a debate add value to the conversation?

A calm and thoughtful response is always better than an impulsive reaction.

b. Acknowledge Constructive Criticism

When someone offers valid feedback, acknowledging it shows professionalism and maturity. Even if you don't fully agree, you can thank them for their perspective. Examples of good responses include:

- *"I appreciate your feedback! I'll consider this for future posts."*

- *"That's a good point. I'll look into it and update my content if needed."*

Such responses encourage respectful discussions and demonstrate that you are open to learning.

c. Clarify Misunderstandings

Sometimes, negative comments stem from misinterpretations of your post. If someone criticizes you based on incorrect assumptions, politely clarify your position. For example:

- *"I see your point, but my argument was actually referring to a different aspect of the topic."*

- *"I think there's been a misunderstanding. What I meant was..."*

Providing context can prevent further negativity and foster meaningful discussions.

d. Use Humor to Diffuse Tension

Humor can sometimes turn a negative interaction into a positive one. If someone is being mildly rude or sarcastic, responding with a lighthearted joke can de-escalate the situation. However, this approach requires careful judgment—some people may misinterpret humor as dismissiveness.

For example, if someone comments, *"Wow, what a dumb take,"* you might respond with:

- *"Dumb takes are my specialty!"* (Followed by an actual explanation if needed.)

This keeps things lighthearted while maintaining control of the conversation.

e. Know When to Ignore or Block

Not all negative comments deserve a response. If someone is clearly trolling or being intentionally rude, the best action is to ignore them. Engaging with trolls only gives them more attention and encourages further negativity.

X provides tools to help you manage interactions:

- **Mute:** This allows you to stop seeing someone's replies without blocking them. They won't know they've been muted.

- **Block:** If someone is persistently negative or harassing you, blocking them removes their ability to interact with your posts.

- **Report:** If a comment is abusive, threatening, or violates X's policies, you can report it for review.

Ignoring negativity often frustrates trolls, as their goal is to provoke a reaction.

3. Protecting Your Mental Well-Being

Constant exposure to negativity can take a toll on your mental health. Here are some strategies to protect yourself:

a. Limit Your Time on X

If you find yourself stressed by negative interactions, take breaks from social media. Set specific times for checking notifications instead of constantly refreshing your feed.

b. Focus on Supportive Communities

Engage more with people who provide positive and constructive discussions. Following like-minded users and participating in encouraging conversations can balance out negativity.

c. Develop a Thick Skin

Not everyone will agree with you, and that's okay. Learn to differentiate between valuable feedback and meaningless negativity. The more you grow on X, the more criticism you will receive—view it as part of the journey.

d. Seek Support if Needed

If online negativity becomes overwhelming, talk to a friend, mentor, or professional for guidance. Remember that social media is just one part of your life—it doesn't define you.

4. Case Studies: Handling Criticism Successfully

To illustrate these principles, let's look at a few real-world examples of how well-known personalities and brands handle criticism on X:

a. Elon Musk and Public Disagreements

Elon Musk, CEO of Tesla and SpaceX, often receives criticism on X. Instead of reacting aggressively, he sometimes uses humor or provides clarifications. However, there are times when his responses escalate conflicts, showing the risks of emotional engagement.

b. Customer Service Accounts and Complaint Handling

Many brands, such as airlines or tech companies, receive complaints daily. The best-managed accounts respond professionally, acknowledge issues, and offer solutions rather than becoming defensive.

c. Influencers Who Turn Criticism into Growth

Many influencers use negative feedback to improve their content. Some even create follow-up posts addressing valid concerns, which strengthens their credibility and engagement.

Conclusion

Handling online criticism is an essential skill for anyone looking to build a presence on X. While negativity is inevitable, responding with professionalism, humor, or simply ignoring the noise can help you maintain a positive reputation. By distinguishing between constructive feedback and trolling, choosing when to engage, and protecting your mental well-being, you can continue growing without being weighed down by negativity.

In the next section, we will explore **"5.4.2 Managing Block and Mute Functions,"** where we'll discuss practical ways to filter and control interactions on X effectively.

5.4.2 Managing Block and Mute Functions

The internet can be an amazing place for communication and engagement, but it also comes with challenges, such as trolls and negative comments. X (Twitter) provides users with tools to manage their interactions and maintain a positive experience on the platform. Two of the most effective features for handling unwanted interactions are the **Block** and **Mute** functions. These tools allow you to control who can interact with you and help you curate a better experience on X (Twitter).

This section will guide you through how to use these features effectively, when to apply them, and best practices for managing your online presence while maintaining a professional or personal brand.

1. Understanding the Block and Mute Functions

Before diving into how to use these features, it's important to understand their key differences:

- **Blocking**: When you block someone on X (Twitter), they will no longer be able to view your tweets, follow you, or interact with your content. They also cannot send you direct messages. Essentially, blocking completely removes a person from your X (Twitter) experience.

- **Muting**: Muting allows you to stop seeing someone's tweets on your timeline without unfollowing or blocking them. The muted person does not know they have been muted, and they can still engage with your content if they follow you.

Both tools serve different purposes, and knowing when to use each can help you maintain a more enjoyable and productive experience on the platform.

2. How to Block Users on X (Twitter)

Blocking is a strong measure to prevent unwanted interactions. If someone is harassing you, spamming your tweets, or being excessively negative, blocking may be the best solution.

Step-by-Step Guide to Blocking a User

1. **Go to the User's Profile**

   o Click on the profile of the person you want to block.

2. **Open the Options Menu**

   o Click the three-dot menu (⋮) on their profile page.

3. **Select "Block"**

   o Choose the "Block" option from the dropdown menu.

4. **Confirm the Action**

   o A confirmation message will appear, explaining that the person will no longer be able to follow or interact with you. Click **Confirm Block** to finalize the action.

What Happens When You Block Someone?

- The blocked user cannot see your tweets (unless they are logged out or using another account).

- They cannot mention, reply to, or message you.

- They will automatically be removed from your followers, and you will also stop following them.

- If they try to visit your profile, they will see a message stating that they have been blocked.

How to Unblock a User

If you ever change your mind and want to unblock someone:

1. Go to **Settings and Privacy > Privacy and Safety > Blocked Accounts**.

2. Find the user in the list and click **Unblock** next to their name.

Blocking is useful for dealing with harassment, spam, or persistent negativity, but it should be used wisely to avoid unnecessary conflicts.

3. How to Mute Users on X (Twitter)

Muting is a great option when you want to stop seeing someone's tweets but don't want to block them entirely. This is useful for avoiding negativity, preventing distractions, or managing an overwhelming feed without unfollowing people.

Step-by-Step Guide to Muting a User

1. **Find the User or Tweet You Want to Mute**

   o You can mute an entire account or just specific conversations.

2. **Click the Three-Dot Menu (⋮)**

   o If you are muting a user, go to their profile and click the three dots.

   o If you are muting a tweet, click the three-dot menu on the specific tweet.

3. **Select "Mute"**

   o From the dropdown menu, select **Mute @username**.

4. **Confirm the Action**

   o A notification will confirm that you have muted the user.

What Happens When You Mute Someone?

- You will no longer see their tweets on your timeline.

- They can still follow, mention, and reply to you.

- They will **not** know that they have been muted.

- You can still visit their profile and interact with their content if you choose to.

How to Unmute a User

1. Go to **Settings and Privacy** > **Privacy and Safety** > **Muted Accounts**.

2. Find the user in the list and click **Unmute** next to their name.

Muting is a great tool for avoiding unnecessary conflicts while still keeping your social connections intact.

4. Muting Notifications for Specific Conversations

Sometimes, you may want to mute a specific conversation rather than an entire user. This is useful when a tweet you engaged with is getting excessive replies or when you're included in a group discussion that doesn't interest you.

How to Mute a Conversation

1. **Go to the Tweet or Notification**

    o Open the tweet or reply chain that you want to mute.

2. **Click the Three-Dot Menu (⋮)**

    o Find the three dots at the top right corner of the tweet.

3. **Select "Mute This Conversation"**

    o This will stop further notifications from this thread.

4. **Confirm the Action**

    o A confirmation will appear to let you know that you will no longer receive alerts from the conversation.

Muting conversations is useful for keeping your notifications manageable without blocking or muting entire accounts.

5. Best Practices for Managing Your X (Twitter) Experience

Using the block and mute functions strategically can help you create a positive experience on X (Twitter). Here are some best practices to consider:

When to Block vs. Mute

Situation	Block	Mute
Harassment or abuse	✓	✗
Spam or bots	✓	✗
Persistent trolling	✓	✗
Annoying but not harmful tweets	✗	✓
Overwhelming content from a friend or colleague	✗	✓

Additional Tips for Managing Negativity

- **Avoid engaging with trolls.** Many negative users thrive on attention. Ignoring them can be the best response.

- **Use X (Twitter) privacy settings.** Consider adjusting who can reply to your tweets and limiting notifications from unknown users.

- **Regularly review your muted and blocked lists.** Sometimes, situations change, and you may want to remove someone from your mute or block list.

- **Report abusive behavior.** If someone is harassing or threatening you, report them to X (Twitter) in addition to blocking them.

6. Conclusion

Blocking and muting are essential tools for maintaining a positive experience on X (Twitter). While blocking is best for dealing with harassment and persistent negativity, muting is a more subtle way to filter content without severing connections. By understanding when and how to use these features, you can create a safer and more enjoyable social media experience.

Managing negativity effectively allows you to focus on meaningful interactions, grow your presence, and enjoy the benefits of social media without unnecessary stress. Use these tools wisely, and remember that you control your online experience.

CHAPTER V
Monetizing and Advertising on X (Twitter)

6.1 Monetization Options

6.1.1 X (Twitter) Creator Program

As social media platforms evolve, they offer more opportunities for content creators to monetize their work. X (formerly Twitter) is no exception. The **X Creator Program** is designed to help users earn money from their content by leveraging various monetization features such as ad revenue sharing, tips, and subscriptions. If you're an active user who engages audiences with valuable, entertaining, or informative content, this program can be a great way to turn your passion into income.

This section explores how the **X Creator Program** works, its eligibility criteria, and strategies to maximize your earnings.

What is the X Creator Program?

The **X Creator Program** is an initiative by X (Twitter) that allows content creators to generate revenue from their tweets, interactions, and community engagement. The program provides multiple income streams, including:

- **Ad Revenue Sharing** – Creators earn a share of the revenue from ads displayed in replies to their posts.

- **Tips and Donations** – Users can send money directly to their favorite creators.

- **Subscriptions (Super Follows)** – Followers can subscribe to exclusive content for a monthly fee.

These monetization options make X (Twitter) an attractive platform for influencers, educators, entertainers, and business professionals who create high-quality content.

Eligibility Requirements for the X Creator Program

Not everyone can immediately enroll in the **X Creator Program**—there are specific requirements that users must meet to qualify. These may vary depending on your region and the specific monetization method, but the general criteria include:

1. Account Age and Activity

- Your X (Twitter) account should be at least **three months old**.
- You must have a **consistent posting history** with engaging content.

2. Follower Count

- You need at least **500 followers** to be eligible for most monetization features.
- For ad revenue sharing, a higher follower count (e.g., 10,000+) may be required.

3. Engagement Metrics

- A minimum of **5 million impressions** on your tweets in the past **three months** (for ad revenue sharing).
- Active engagement (likes, replies, and retweets) is essential for eligibility.

4. Compliance with X (Twitter) Policies

- You must follow **X's content policies**—this includes avoiding spam, misinformation, and harmful content.
- Your account **must not have repeated violations** or be under restrictions due to misconduct.

How to Join the X Creator Program

If you meet the eligibility criteria, joining the program is straightforward. Here's how you can sign up:

1. **Go to X (Twitter) Settings**

   o   Navigate to the **Monetization** section under account settings.

2. **Apply for the X Creator Program**

   o   You may need to verify your eligibility before proceeding.

   o   Agree to X's **Creator Terms and Conditions**.

3. **Set Up Payment Details**

   o   Link your account to a **payment service** (such as Stripe or PayPal) to receive earnings.

   o   Ensure your payment details match the region you are applying from.

4. **Enable Monetization Features**

   o   Depending on your eligibility, enable features like **Ad Revenue Sharing, Tips, or Subscriptions**.

   o   Customize your **subscription pricing** if applicable.

5. **Start Creating Monetizable Content**

   o   Once approved, your content will begin generating revenue based on engagement.

Revenue Streams in the X Creator Program

The **X Creator Program** offers multiple revenue streams, allowing users to maximize their earnings based on their content type and audience.

1. Ad Revenue Sharing

One of the most attractive aspects of the **X Creator Program** is **ad revenue sharing**. When ads appear in the replies to your tweets, you receive a percentage of the earnings.

How It Works:

- Ads are automatically inserted in the reply sections of your high-engagement tweets.

- You earn **a share of the ad revenue** based on impressions and clicks.

- Higher engagement leads to **more ad impressions**, increasing revenue potential.

Best Practices to Maximize Ad Revenue:

- Post **engaging tweets** that encourage replies and discussions.

- Participate in trending topics and conversations.

- Use images, videos, and GIFs to enhance visibility.

- Avoid controversial or sensitive topics that may limit ad placements.

2. Tips and Donations

The **Tips feature** allows followers to send **small monetary contributions** directly to their favorite creators. This is ideal for:

- Artists

- Writers

- Educators

- Journalists

- Entertainers

How to Enable Tips:

- Go to **Monetization Settings** and activate the Tips feature.

- Link a payment method (e.g., **Cash App, PayPal, or Bitcoin Wallet**).

- A **"Tip Jar"** icon will appear on your profile, allowing followers to send donations.

Strategies to Increase Tips:

- Engage with your followers and express appreciation.

- Share **behind-the-scenes** content or exclusive insights.

- Politely remind followers that tips help support your content.

3. Subscriptions (Super Follows)

With **Super Follows**, creators can offer exclusive content to **subscribers** for a monthly fee. This feature is similar to Patreon but integrated directly into X (Twitter).

How to Set Up Super Follows:

- Go to **Monetization Settings** and enable **Super Follows**.
- Choose a **subscription price** (typically $2.99, $4.99, or $9.99 per month).
- Create **exclusive content** that only subscribers can access.

Content Ideas for Super Followers:

- **Exclusive tweets** with premium insights.
- **Q&A sessions** for subscribers.
- **Early access** to your content or announcements.
- **Subscriber-only threads** discussing niche topics.

Tips for Growing Your Subscriber Base:

- Offer **valuable and unique content** that's worth subscribing to.
- Promote your **Super Follow option** regularly.
- Engage with subscribers through **personalized shoutouts** or exclusive chats.

Challenges and Considerations in the X Creator Program

While the **X Creator Program** offers exciting monetization opportunities, it also comes with challenges:

1. Competition for Engagement

- Many creators are competing for attention—finding a niche can help.
- Engaging **authentically** with followers increases retention.

2. Algorithm Changes

- X (Twitter) updates its algorithm frequently, affecting content visibility.

- Staying updated with **platform changes** is crucial for long-term success.

3. Content Consistency

- Posting **high-quality content consistently** is key to maintaining monetization eligibility.

- Scheduling tools can help manage your posting routine.

4. Payment and Regional Restrictions

- Some monetization features are **not available in all countries**.

- Payment processing times vary depending on the method used.

Final Thoughts

The **X Creator Program** is an excellent opportunity for social media users to turn their influence into income. Whether through **ad revenue, tips, or subscriptions**, creators can build sustainable earnings with the right strategy. However, success requires **consistency, engagement, and adaptability** to platform changes.

If you're considering monetizing your content on X (Twitter), start by focusing on **growing your audience**, creating **valuable content**, and staying **active in discussions**. Over time, these efforts can translate into a profitable and rewarding social media presence.

6.1.2 Subscriptions and Super Follows

As social media platforms evolve, they are providing more opportunities for creators to monetize their content and engage with their audience in meaningful ways. X (formerly Twitter) has introduced two key features for monetization: **Subscriptions** and **Super Follows**. These tools allow creators to earn revenue directly from their followers by offering exclusive content, perks, and a more personalized experience.

In this section, we will explore how Subscriptions and Super Follows work, their benefits, how to set them up, and best practices for maximizing earnings.

Understanding Subscriptions and Super Follows

Subscriptions and Super Follows are **premium content features** on X that let followers pay a **monthly fee** to access exclusive content and benefits from their favorite creators.

- **Subscriptions** allow creators to offer exclusive tweets, interactions, and perks to subscribers who pay a monthly fee.

- **Super Follows** (now integrated into Subscriptions) originally allowed followers to support their favorite accounts by paying for extra content.

Both of these features are designed to help **content creators, influencers, and businesses** build sustainable revenue while strengthening their relationship with their most loyal followers.

How These Features Benefit Creators

1. **Recurring Revenue Stream** – Instead of relying only on ads or brand deals, creators can generate **consistent income** from dedicated followers.

2. **Stronger Community Engagement** – By offering **exclusive content**, creators can build a **tighter-knit community** of loyal supporters.

3. **Greater Creative Freedom** – Without depending solely on sponsors, creators can focus on **authentic and engaging** content.

4. **Monetizing Expertise and Influence** – Experts, thought leaders, and niche influencers can **monetize their knowledge** through exclusive insights and interactions.

Eligibility Requirements for Subscriptions and Super Follows

Not everyone can immediately start using Subscriptions. To **qualify**, X has set specific requirements:

- **Age**: Must be **18 years or older**.

- **Followers**: Must have at least **500 followers** (subject to change).

- **Activity**: Must have been active on X for **at least 3 months**.

- **Content Compliance**: Must follow **X's content policies** and monetization rules.

- **Region Availability**: Feature must be **available in the creator's country** (check X's official support pages for updates).

Creators meeting these criteria can **apply through the X app** under the monetization settings.

How to Set Up Subscriptions and Super Follows

Step 1: Apply for the Program

1. Open the **X app** and go to **Settings and Privacy**.

2. Navigate to **Monetization > Subscriptions**.

3. If eligible, click **Apply** and follow the on-screen instructions.

4. Once approved, set up **pricing tiers** and define the benefits for your subscribers.

Step 2: Choose a Subscription Price

Creators can choose from **several pricing options**, such as **$2.99, $4.99, or $9.99 per month**. Higher tiers allow for premium perks.

Step 3: Define Exclusive Benefits

To encourage followers to subscribe, creators should offer **valuable, unique content** such as:

- **Subscriber-only tweets** (behind-the-scenes content, insights, or special announcements).

- **Exclusive live interactions** (Q&A sessions, AMA events, private Spaces).

- **Early access to content** (such as articles, videos, or updates).

- **Subscriber badges** (to recognize and highlight paying members).

Step 4: Promote Your Subscription

1. **Announce the feature** – Let followers know about the subscription and its benefits.

2. **Create a pinned post** – Pin a tweet explaining the exclusive content.

3. **Engage with subscribers regularly** – Provide consistent value to maintain their support.

Best Practices for Maximizing Revenue

1. Offer Exclusive, High-Value Content

Subscribers need to feel that their **investment is worth it**. Provide:

- **Exclusive insights** or premium industry knowledge.
- **Behind-the-scenes looks** into projects or personal life.
- **Engaging discussions** tailored for your premium audience.

2. Interact with Subscribers Regularly

Building a strong **community feel** helps with retention. Ways to engage:

- **Reply to subscriber tweets** to make them feel valued.
- **Host monthly live Q&A sessions** to keep interactions personal.
- **Create polls and discussions** to encourage engagement.

3. Experiment with Different Content Types

Test various formats to see what resonates best:

- **Text-based insights** for industry experts.
- **Video messages or live interactions** for influencers.
- **Exclusive polls or discussions** for community building.

4. Promote Your Subscription Smartly

To attract more subscribers, integrate promotional efforts into your content strategy:

- Use **CTA (Call to Action)** in tweets to remind followers about your subscription.
- Occasionally **showcase snippets** of premium content to tease non-subscribers.
- Offer **limited-time bonuses** for new subscribers.

5. Retain Subscribers with Consistency

Regularly delivering valuable content ensures people **stay subscribed**. To achieve this:

- Plan a **content calendar** for your subscribers.

- Communicate clearly about **updates and new perks**.

- Show appreciation for long-term subscribers (e.g., shoutouts).

Common Mistakes to Avoid

1. Ignoring Subscribers

Failing to interact with paying members can lead to **cancellations**.

2. Lack of Exclusive Value

If subscribers don't feel they're getting **unique, high-value content**, they won't renew.

3. Over-Promoting Without Delivering

Continuously pushing for subscriptions without actually **providing engaging content** can backfire.

4. Setting Prices Too High Without Justification

If you price at $9.99/month, make sure you're offering **premium content**.

The Future of Subscriptions on X

X continues to expand monetization features, with future updates likely to include:

- **More pricing flexibility** for subscriptions.

- **Better tools for engagement** with paying subscribers.

- **Integration with other revenue streams** (e.g., paid Spaces, ticketed events).

As the platform evolves, **content creators and businesses** who effectively use Subscriptions and Super Follows can create **sustainable revenue streams** while fostering **stronger audience relationships**.

Final Thoughts

Subscriptions and Super Follows on X provide a powerful **monetization tool** for creators, influencers, and businesses. By offering **exclusive content, meaningful interactions, and unique perks**, users can build **a loyal community** and generate **consistent income**.

However, success depends on **delivering value, maintaining engagement, and promoting the feature strategically**. By following the best practices outlined in this section, you can **turn your presence on X into a profitable venture** while strengthening your bond with your most dedicated followers.

6.2 Running Ads on X (Twitter)

Advertising on X (Twitter) is a powerful way to reach your target audience, boost engagement, and promote your brand, product, or service. With its vast user base and highly customizable ad options, X allows businesses and individuals to create ad campaigns tailored to their specific goals.

In this section, we will focus on **setting up a Twitter Ads campaign**, guiding you through the process from start to finish.

6.2.1 Setting Up a Twitter Ads Campaign

Running a successful Twitter Ads campaign involves careful planning, proper audience targeting, and continuous optimization. Below is a step-by-step guide to setting up your first Twitter Ads campaign.

Step 1: Access Twitter Ads Manager

To start advertising on X (Twitter), you need to access **Twitter Ads Manager**, the platform's official advertising dashboard.

How to Access Twitter Ads Manager:

1. **Log into Your Twitter Account** – Use the account you want to advertise from.

2. **Go to Twitter Ads** – Visit ads.twitter.com in your browser.

3. **Select Your Country and Time Zone** – Twitter will use this information for billing and reporting.

4. **Click on "Get Started"** – This will take you to the main Twitter Ads dashboard.

Once inside, you will see options for campaign creation, billing, analytics, and more.

Step 2: Choose Your Campaign Objective

Twitter Ads are designed to help you achieve specific goals. The platform offers several **campaign objectives** depending on what you want to accomplish.

Common Twitter Ad Objectives:

- **Awareness** – Increase visibility by maximizing impressions.
- **Engagement** – Get more likes, replies, and retweets.
- **Followers** – Attract new followers to your profile.
- **Website Clicks or Conversions** – Drive traffic to your website or landing page.
- **App Installs** – Promote app downloads.
- **Video Views** – Increase views on your videos.

💡 *Tip:* If you're new to Twitter Ads, start with "Engagement" or "Website Clicks" to drive interaction and traffic.

Once you select your campaign objective, click **"Next"** to proceed.

Step 3: Define Your Campaign Details

After selecting your objective, you will be asked to enter **campaign details** including:

- **Campaign Name** – Choose a descriptive name for your campaign.
- **Funding Source** – Add or select a payment method.
- **Daily or Lifetime Budget** – Set your budget limits.
- **Start and End Date** – Schedule when your ads will run.

💡 *Tip:* Start with a **small budget** to test different strategies before scaling up.

Step 4: Create an Ad Group

Twitter Ads organizes campaigns into **ad groups** that help you target different audiences. You can create multiple ad groups within one campaign to test different strategies.

Key Ad Group Settings:

- **Ad Group Name** – Label your ad group for easy tracking.
- **Bid Type** – Choose between *automatic* (Twitter sets the bid) or *manual* (you control the cost per engagement).
- **Targeting Options** – Define who will see your ad.

💡 *Tip:* For beginners, use **automatic bidding** to optimize costs while learning.

Step 5: Define Your Target Audience

Twitter Ads allows **precise audience targeting** to reach the right people.

Main Targeting Options:

1. **Demographics**
   - Location: Target users based on country, state, city, or ZIP code.
   - Age: Specify age ranges for your audience.
   - Gender: Choose male, female, or all genders.

2. **Interests and Behavior**
   - Target users based on what they tweet about, like, or follow.
   - Use behavioral insights to focus on active buyers, influencers, or industry professionals.

3. **Keywords and Hashtags**
   - Target users who have tweeted or engaged with specific keywords.

- o Example: If you are promoting a fitness app, target users who tweet about "workout" or "fitness goals."

4. **Follower Lookalike Audiences**

- o Target users similar to the followers of a specific account.

- o Example: If you want to reach marketing professionals, you could target followers of @HubSpot or @MarketingLand.

5. **Custom Audiences**

- o Upload your email list or phone numbers to target existing customers.

- o Retarget users who have previously interacted with your brand.

💡 *Tip:* Combine multiple targeting options for a **highly refined audience** that is more likely to convert.

Step 6: Choose Your Ad Placement

Twitter Ads allows you to display your ads in different locations:

- • **Home Timelines** – Your ad appears as a promoted tweet in users' feeds.

- • **Search Results** – Ads appear when users search for specific keywords.

- • **User Profiles** – Ads appear on profile pages.

- • **Twitter Audience Platform** – Extend your ads beyond Twitter to external apps and websites.

💡 *Tip: Home Timeline ads* tend to generate higher engagement as they blend naturally into users' feeds.

Step 7: Select Your Ad Format

Twitter Ads offers several **ad formats** to showcase your content:

1. **Promoted Tweets** – Appear like regular tweets but with increased visibility.

2. **Promoted Accounts** – Encourage users to follow your account.

3. **Promoted Trends** – Feature your hashtag at the top of the trending section.

4. **Video Ads** – Promote videos with autoplay functionality.

5. **Carousel Ads** – Show multiple images or videos in a swipeable format.

💡 *Tip:* Use **high-quality visuals** and engaging copy to make your ads stand out.

Step 8: Set Your Budget and Bidding Strategy

Twitter Ads allows you to control how much you spend by setting:

- **Daily Budget** – Maximum amount you want to spend per day.

- **Total Budget** – The total amount allocated for the entire campaign.

- **Bid Strategy:**

  o **Automatic Bidding** – Twitter adjusts your bid for the best results.

  o **Maximum Bidding** – Set a limit on how much you're willing to pay per action.

💡 *Tip:* Start with **automatic bidding** to let Twitter optimize your ad spend.

Step 9: Review and Launch Your Campaign

Before launching, double-check:

✓ Campaign objective
✓ Target audience settings
✓ Ad content and format
✓ Budget and bidding strategy

Once everything is set, click **"Launch Campaign"** to start running your ad.

Step 10: Monitor and Optimize Your Campaign

After launching, use **Twitter Ads Analytics** to track performance.

Key Metrics to Monitor:

- **Impressions** – How many times your ad was seen.

- **Engagement Rate** – The percentage of users who interacted with your ad.

- **Click-Through Rate (CTR)** – How many users clicked on your ad.

- **Conversion Rate** – How many users completed a desired action (e.g., website visit, purchase).

💡 *Tip:* If engagement is low, **test different ad creatives, targeting, and copy** to improve results.

Final Thoughts

Setting up a **Twitter Ads campaign** is straightforward, but success requires **testing and optimization**. By following this step-by-step guide, you can create highly effective campaigns that boost engagement, drive traffic, and maximize ROI.

In the next section, we will dive deeper into **understanding different ad formats** and how to choose the best one for your business.

6.2.2 Understanding Different Ad Formats

Advertising on X (formerly Twitter) is a powerful way to increase visibility, drive engagement, and promote products or services. To create a successful ad campaign, it's essential to understand the different ad formats available and how to use them effectively. This section will explore the various ad formats on X, their advantages, use cases, and best practices.

---

1. Introduction to X (Twitter) Ad Formats

X offers a variety of advertising options that cater to different marketing objectives, such as brand awareness, engagement, website traffic, lead generation, and conversions. Each ad format serves a unique purpose and can be tailored to target specific audiences. Advertisers can choose from the following types of ads:

1. **Promoted Ads** – Regular tweets that appear in users' feeds as sponsored content.

2. **Follower Ads** – Ads designed to increase an account's follower base.

3. **Amplify Pre-Roll Ads** – Video ads that appear before premium video content.

4. **Twitter Takeover Ads** – Premium ads that take over prime real estate on the platform.

5. **Twitter Live and Video Ads** – Engaging video formats designed to capture attention.

6. **Dynamic Product Ads (DPA)** – Automated product ads based on user behavior.

Each of these formats has specific advantages, and choosing the right one depends on the campaign's goal.

2. Promoted Ads

What Are Promoted Ads?

Promoted Ads function like regular tweets but are paid to appear in users' feeds, search results, and profiles. They help increase visibility and engagement by reaching a broader audience.

Types of Promoted Ads

1. **Promoted Text Ads** – Standard tweets that appear with a "Promoted" label.

2. **Promoted Image Ads** – Tweets with high-quality images designed to grab attention.

3. **Promoted Video Ads** – Short videos that autoplay in users' feeds.

4. **Promoted GIF Ads** – Animated images that stand out in a scrolling timeline.

5. **Promoted Carousel Ads** – A multi-image or multi-video format allowing interactive storytelling.

Best Use Cases for Promoted Ads

- Driving website traffic

- Increasing tweet engagement

- Promoting a new product or service

- Generating app installs

Best Practices for Promoted Ads

- Use high-quality visuals to capture attention.

- Keep text concise and engaging.

- Include a strong call-to-action (CTA).

- Optimize tweets for mobile users.

3. Follower Ads

What Are Follower Ads?

Follower Ads (formerly known as Promoted Accounts) help brands increase their follower base by displaying their profile in users' feeds, the "Who to Follow" section, and search results. These ads encourage users to follow an account by highlighting its value proposition.

Best Use Cases for Follower Ads

- Building brand credibility

- Growing an audience for future organic engagement

- Attracting potential customers or fans

Best Practices for Follower Ads

- Craft a compelling bio that showcases the brand's purpose.

- Use a high-quality profile image and banner.

- Ensure the first pinned tweet is engaging and relevant.

4. Amplify Pre-Roll Ads

What Are Amplify Pre-Roll Ads?

Amplify Pre-Roll Ads are video advertisements that play before premium video content from X's media partners, such as news outlets and sports networks. They function similarly to YouTube pre-roll ads.

Best Use Cases for Amplify Pre-Roll Ads

- Increasing brand awareness

- Associating with premium content creators

- Driving video views

Best Practices for Amplify Pre-Roll Ads

- Keep videos under 6 seconds for maximum retention.

- Include captions for better accessibility.

- Ensure brand messaging appears in the first few seconds.

5. Twitter Takeover Ads

What Are Twitter Takeover Ads?

Takeover Ads offer premium placements for advertisers who want maximum exposure. These ads dominate the top spots on X's homepage, trends list, and user timelines.

Types of Takeover Ads

1. **Timeline Takeover** – The first ad users see when they open X.

2. **Trend Takeover** – A promoted trending topic appearing at the top of the Trends section.

3. **Trend Takeover+** – An enhanced version with rich media assets like GIFs and videos.

Best Use Cases for Twitter Takeover Ads

- Launching a new product or service

- Promoting major events or campaigns

- Generating viral conversations

Best Practices for Twitter Takeover Ads

- Use eye-catching visuals and concise messaging.

- Align ad campaigns with trending topics or major events.

- Optimize for both desktop and mobile viewing.

6. Twitter Live and Video Ads

What Are Twitter Live and Video Ads?

These ads allow brands to stream live video content or post video ads within user feeds. Video ads are one of the most engaging formats on the platform.

Best Use Cases for Twitter Live and Video Ads

- Hosting Q&A sessions and live events

- Promoting product demos

- Enhancing storytelling through dynamic visuals

Best Practices for Twitter Live and Video Ads

- Use compelling thumbnails to attract clicks.

- Ensure high-quality video production.

- Add captions to make content accessible.

7. Dynamic Product Ads (DPA)

What Are Dynamic Product Ads?

DPAs are automated ads that retarget users based on their previous interactions with a brand's website or app. These ads dynamically generate product recommendations tailored to individual users.

Best Use Cases for Dynamic Product Ads

- Retargeting abandoned cart users

- Increasing e-commerce conversions

- Promoting seasonal sales and discounts

Best Practices for Dynamic Product Ads

- Personalize ad content based on user behavior.

- Test different product variations for better engagement.

- Optimize product images and descriptions.

8. Choosing the Right Ad Format for Your Campaign

With multiple ad formats available, selecting the right one depends on the campaign's goal. Here's a quick guide:

Objective	Best Ad Format
Increase brand awareness	Promoted Ads, Twitter Takeover, Amplify Pre-Roll Ads
Drive website traffic	Promoted Image/Video Ads, Carousel Ads
Grow followers	Follower Ads
Boost engagement	Promoted Video Ads, Twitter Live Ads
Retarget potential customers	Dynamic Product Ads

9. Budgeting and Optimizing Ad Performance on X (Twitter)

Running ads on X (formerly Twitter) can be highly effective, but to maximize your return on investment (ROI), you need to understand budgeting strategies and optimization techniques. This section will guide you through setting up an effective ad budget, optimizing performance, and measuring success.

Understanding Ad Budgeting on X (Twitter)

When setting up an ad campaign on X, you have flexibility in controlling how much you spend. The platform offers different budgeting options to match various business needs.

Types of Budgets on X Ads

1. **Daily Budget** – The amount you're willing to spend per day.

   o Ensures steady spending throughout the campaign.

   o Best for ongoing awareness campaigns.

2. **Total Budget (Lifetime Budget)** – A fixed amount spent over the entire campaign duration.

   o Ideal for short-term promotions.

   o Prevents overspending.

3. **Bid-Based Budgeting** – You set the maximum bid per engagement, impression, or conversion.

   o Offers flexibility in competitive markets.

   o Works well for optimizing cost-per-action (CPA).

How X (Twitter) Ad Bidding Works

X Ads operate on an auction system, meaning the platform determines which ads get shown based on:

- **Bid Amount** – How much you're willing to pay per action (click, impression, engagement).

- **Ad Quality Score** – The relevance and engagement potential of your ad.

- **Competition** – The number of advertisers bidding for the same audience.

To get the best results, balance a competitive bid with high-quality, engaging content.

2. Key Strategies for Optimizing Ad Performance

Simply running an ad isn't enough—you need to optimize it for better reach and engagement.

Choosing the Right Target Audience

X Ads allow you to target users based on:

- **Demographics** – Age, gender, location.

- **Interests** – Topics and hashtags they engage with.

- **Behavior** – Past interactions, device type, and online activities.

- **Custom Audiences** – Upload email lists or retarget website visitors.

Optimization Tip: Use A/B testing with different audience segments to see which performs best.

Writing High-Performing Ad Copy

- **Keep It Concise** – Tweets have limited characters, so make every word count.

- **Use Strong Call-to-Actions (CTAs)** – Examples: "Shop Now," "Learn More," "Sign Up Today."

- **Leverage Urgency** – Limited-time offers work well (e.g., "Only 24 Hours Left!").

- **Incorporate Keywords** – Align ad copy with trending topics and hashtags.

Enhancing Ad Creatives

- **Use High-Quality Images and Videos** – Posts with visuals get **3x more engagement**.

- **Optimize for Mobile** – Over **80% of users access X from mobile devices**.

- **Test Different Formats** – Static images vs. GIFs vs. videos.

Optimization Tip: Try different versions of your ad (A/B testing) to see what resonates most.

Leveraging Ad Scheduling for Maximum Impact

Schedule ads during **peak engagement hours** based on your target audience. Studies show:

- **Best times to post ads**:
    - B2B businesses: **Weekdays (9 AM – 12 PM EST)**
    - B2C businesses: **Evenings & weekends (7 PM – 10 PM EST)**

3. Measuring Ad Performance and Adjusting Strategies

Key Metrics to Track

- **Impressions** – Number of times your ad is seen.

- **Engagement Rate** – Percentage of people interacting with your ad (likes, retweets, comments).

- **Click-Through Rate (CTR)** – The percentage of users clicking on your ad.

- **Cost Per Click (CPC)** – The amount paid for each click.

- **Conversion Rate** – Percentage of users completing a desired action (sign-up, purchase).

Using Twitter Analytics to Improve Performance

X Ads provides detailed analytics to help refine your strategy. Key reports include:

- **Audience Insights** – Understand who is engaging with your ads.

- **Ad Performance Dashboard** – Compare multiple ad campaigns.

- **Conversion Tracking** – Measure ad impact on website visits and purchases.

Optimization Tip: If an ad isn't performing well, tweak **either the audience targeting, creative, or copy**, but not all at once.

---

4. Budget Optimization Techniques for Maximum ROI

Start with a Small Test Budget

Before committing large amounts, test different ad formats, creatives, and audiences.

Example: Start with **$10–$20/day** for the first week and scale up based on performance.

Adjust Spending Based on Performance

If an ad is outperforming others, allocate **more budget** to it and reduce spending on underperforming ads.

Retargeting for Better Conversions

Retarget users who have:

- Visited your website but didn't complete a purchase.

- Engaged with your previous tweets but didn't follow.

Dynamic Product Ads (DPA) and Custom Audiences work well for retargeting.

5. Common Budgeting Mistakes to Avoid

Spending Too Much Without Testing

New advertisers often invest heavily without testing different ad formats. Always **start small** and analyze results.

Ignoring Mobile Optimization

Since most users access X from mobile, ads should be **mobile-friendly** with short text and engaging visuals.

Not Monitoring Ad Performance Regularly

Don't "set and forget" ads. Check performance **daily or weekly** to make necessary adjustments.

Overcomplicating Targeting

Targeting too many filters can **limit reach**. Keep your audience broad at first and refine over time.

6. Conclusion

Budgeting and optimizing ads on X requires **strategy, testing, and continuous improvement**. By setting realistic budgets, refining audience targeting, crafting engaging creatives, and tracking performance metrics, you can maximize your advertising ROI.

Key Takeaways:
✓ Choose the right **budget type** based on your campaign goals.
✓ Optimize **audience targeting** for better engagement.
✓ Use **A/B testing** to find the best-performing ads.
✓ Monitor **key metrics** and adjust your budget accordingly.

To make the budgeting and optimization process clearer, let's walk through a real-world scenario.

Scenario: Promoting a New Online Course

Business: A digital marketing agency, *GrowthBoost*, is launching an online course called *"Twitter Ads Mastery: From Beginner to Expert."*

Goal: Generate **500 course sign-ups** within 30 days.

Budget: $3,000 for the entire campaign.

Target Audience:

- Entrepreneurs, marketers, and business owners.

- Aged **24–40**, located in the **US, UK, and Canada**.

- Interested in **social media marketing, digital advertising, and business growth**.

Step 1: Setting the Right Budgeting Strategy

Budget Allocation

- **$1,000 (33%) for Brand Awareness Ads** – To drive engagement and clicks.

- **$1,500 (50%) for Conversion Ads** – Directing users to the course landing page.

- **$500 (17%) for Retargeting Ads** – Targeting users who visited the website but didn't sign up.

Bidding Strategy

Since the goal is conversions, *GrowthBoost* sets a **maximum bid of $3 per click (CPC)** to remain competitive while maintaining profitability.

Step 2: Choosing the Best Ad Formats

Ad 1: Engaging Video Ad for Brand Awareness

- **Format: Video Ad (15s clip)**

- **Content:** Showcasing testimonials from previous students.

- **Call-to-Action (CTA):** *"Want to master Twitter Ads? Enroll today! 🚀"*

- **Targeting:** Entrepreneurs, marketers, and small business owners.

- **Budget:** $1,000 (Daily spend: ~$33 over 30 days).

☞ **Why?** Video ads **increase engagement by 50%** compared to static ads.

Ad 2: Conversion-Focused Image Ad

- **Format: Single Image Ad**

- **Content:** A well-designed banner showing a limited-time offer:

  - **"Get 50% Off – Only This Week!"**

- **Call-to-Action (CTA):** *"Sign up now and start learning today!"*

- **Landing Page:** Directs users to the sign-up page.

- **Budget:** $1,500 (Daily spend: ~$50 over 30 days).

☞ **Why?** Adding a discount **creates urgency and drives conversions**.

Ad 3: Retargeting Carousel Ad

- **Format: Carousel Ad (Multiple images of course benefits & instructor intro)**

- **Targeting:** Users who clicked on previous ads but didn't sign up.

- **Budget:** $500 (Daily spend: ~$16 over 30 days).

☞ **Why?** Retargeting users who showed interest **increases conversions by 70%**.

Step 3: Optimizing the Campaign for Better Results

1. A/B Testing (First 10 Days)

- Test **two different CTAs:**

  - **Ad 1A:** "Sign up now!"

- o **Ad 1B:** "Start learning today – enroll now!"
- Test **two different ad images** for the conversion ad.
- Based on the best-performing version, shift more budget to that ad.

☞ **Result:**

- *Ad 1B had a **15% higher click-through rate (CTR)** than Ad 1A.*
- *Image Ad with "Limited-Time Offer" outperformed the other by **25%.***

✅ **Action Taken:** Allocated more budget to the winning variations.

---

2. Adjusting Targeting Based on Engagement Metrics

- Initially, the ads targeted **entrepreneurs, marketers, and small business owners**.
- Twitter Analytics showed **marketers had the highest engagement rate (CTR of 4.5%)**.
- Adjusted ad spend to focus more on this segment.

✅ **Action Taken:**

- Reduced targeting for **entrepreneurs** (lower engagement).
- Increased budget for **marketers** (higher conversion rate).

---

3. Using Ad Scheduling to Maximize Engagement

- Twitter data showed **peak engagement hours were 9 AM – 12 PM and 7 PM – 10 PM (EST).**
- Scheduled ads to run only during these times instead of 24/7.

✅ **Action Taken:**

- Improved **engagement rate by 20%** just by adjusting posting times.

Final Results After 30 Days

Metric	Before Optimization	After Optimization
Click-Through Rate (CTR)	2.8%	**5.2%** 🚀
Cost Per Click (CPC)	$3.00	**$2.10** ✅
Total Sign-Ups	320	**515** 🎉
ROI	180%	**250%** 📈

Key Takeaways from This Example

1️⃣ **Start with a diverse budget allocation** – Awareness, conversion, and retargeting all play a role.

2️⃣ **Test multiple ad variations** – A/B testing different headlines, images, and CTAs helps find the best-performing ads.

3️⃣ **Refine audience targeting** – Focus on the audience segments that engage the most.

4️⃣ **Use ad scheduling** – Running ads during peak engagement hours boosts performance.

5️⃣ **Monitor and adjust regularly** – Small tweaks can significantly improve results over time.

6.3 Partnering with Brands and Sponsors

6.3.1 How to Find Sponsorship Opportunities

Introduction

Monetizing your presence on X (Twitter) through sponsorships is a powerful way to generate income while sharing content that aligns with your personal brand or business. Whether you are an influencer, a content creator, or a thought leader in your niche, partnering with brands can provide financial rewards and professional growth. However, finding the right sponsorship opportunities requires strategic planning, networking, and an understanding of how brands evaluate potential partners.

In this section, we'll explore different ways to find sponsorship opportunities on X (Twitter), the criteria brands look for in creators, and strategies to pitch yourself effectively.

1. Understanding How Sponsorships Work on X (Twitter)

Before diving into the process of securing sponsorships, it's essential to understand how brands approach partnerships on X (Twitter). Sponsorships generally fall into one of the following categories:

- **Sponsored Tweets** – A brand pays you to post a tweet promoting their product or service.

- **Affiliate Partnerships** – You promote a brand's product and earn a commission for each sale or referral.

- **Long-term Brand Deals** – Ongoing collaborations where you become a brand ambassador.

- **Content Collaborations** – Co-creating content with a brand, such as hosting Twitter Spaces or participating in campaigns.

Each type of sponsorship offers different levels of engagement and financial compensation, so it's important to determine which aligns best with your content strategy.

2. Optimizing Your X (Twitter) Profile for Sponsorships

Before reaching out to brands, ensure your X (Twitter) profile is attractive to potential sponsors. Brands look for creators with a professional, engaging presence. Here are some key elements to focus on:

a) Build a Strong Personal Brand

- Clearly define your niche and expertise. Are you focused on tech, finance, fitness, fashion, or another industry?

- Maintain consistency in your tone, messaging, and content themes.

- Use a professional profile picture and banner that reflect your brand identity.

b) Craft an Engaging Bio

Your bio is the first thing potential sponsors see. Ensure it:

- Clearly states who you are and what you do.

- Highlights any relevant achievements (e.g., "Tech influencer | 50K+ followers | Featured in Forbes").

- Includes a call-to-action (e.g., "DM for collaborations").

c) Maintain High-Quality Content

- Regularly post high-value, engaging content that resonates with your audience.

- Use a mix of text, images, videos, and interactive features like polls.

- Engage with your audience through replies, retweets, and discussions.

d) Showcase Past Collaborations

If you've worked with brands before, highlight them in your tweets, pinned posts, or profile. If you're new to sponsorships, consider promoting products organically to demonstrate your influence.

---

3. Where to Find Sponsorship Opportunities

Finding sponsorships requires proactive effort. Here are some effective ways to connect with brands:

a) Direct Outreach to Brands

One of the best ways to secure sponsorships is to reach out directly to brands that align with your audience. Here's how to do it effectively:

- Identify brands that frequently collaborate with influencers in your niche.

- Follow their official accounts and engage with their content.

- Find the right contact person (social media manager, influencer marketing manager, or PR representative).

- Send a concise, professional pitch (more on this in Section 5).

b) Join Influencer Marketing Platforms

Many brands use influencer marketing platforms to connect with creators. Signing up for these platforms increases your chances of getting sponsorship deals. Some popular platforms include:

- **Upfluence**

- **FameBit (by YouTube, but applicable for Twitter too)**

- **Grapevine**

- **Heepsy**

- **Izea**

These platforms allow you to apply for campaigns and get matched with brands based on your niche and audience size.

c) Engage with Brands Organically

Sometimes, the best way to attract sponsorships is to naturally engage with brands before pitching. Here's how:

- Mention and tag brands in relevant tweets.

- Participate in brand-related discussions and hashtag campaigns.

- Share your experiences with their products in an authentic way.

- Retweet and comment on their posts to increase visibility.

Brands often notice influencers who are already talking about them and may reach out for a formal partnership.

d) Leverage Your Existing Network

- Connect with other influencers in your niche who have sponsorships.

- Ask for referrals or insights on brands that are looking for collaborations.

- Attend industry events (both virtual and in-person) to network with brand representatives.

e) Use Twitter Spaces and Communities

- Hosting or participating in **Twitter Spaces** can attract brand attention.

- Engaging in **Twitter Communities** can increase visibility within your niche.

Brands looking for knowledgeable creators often scout these spaces for potential partnerships.

4. Crafting the Perfect Sponsorship Pitch

Once you've identified a brand to work with, the next step is to pitch yourself effectively. Here's how to craft a compelling proposal:

a) Personalize Your Message

Avoid sending generic emails or DMs. Research the brand and tailor your pitch to show why you're a great fit.

Example introduction:

"Hi [Brand Name], I'm a digital marketing expert with a strong presence on X (Twitter), where I share insights on [your niche]. I've been a fan of your brand and have mentioned your products in my tweets before. I'd love to explore a potential partnership where I can showcase your product to my engaged audience of [follower count] users."

b) Highlight Your Value Proposition

Brands want to know what you can offer. Include:

- Your audience demographics (age, interests, location).

- Your average engagement rate (likes, retweets, replies).

- Past successful collaborations or case studies.

c) Offer Collaboration Ideas

Instead of simply asking for sponsorship, suggest specific campaign ideas:

- A sponsored tweet series.

- A Twitter thread demonstrating product benefits.

- Hosting a Twitter Space discussing the brand's industry.

d) Include Your Media Kit

A media kit makes you look professional. It should include:

- Your bio and niche.

- Key statistics (followers, engagement rate, past sponsorships).

- Content examples.

5. Following Up and Negotiating Sponsorship Deals

After sending your pitch, be prepared to follow up:

- Wait about **one week** before sending a polite follow-up message.

- If they express interest, discuss deliverables, pricing, and expectations.

- Negotiate terms such as exclusivity, content frequency, and compensation.

If a brand declines, ask for feedback and stay open to future opportunities.

Conclusion

Finding sponsorship opportunities on X (Twitter) requires a strategic approach, persistence, and a strong personal brand. By optimizing your profile, engaging with brands, leveraging influencer platforms, and crafting compelling pitches, you can successfully secure sponsorship deals. Remember, authenticity and value-driven content will set you apart from others in your niche.

By following these strategies, you can turn your X (Twitter) presence into a profitable venture and establish long-term partnerships with reputable brands.

6.3.2 Negotiating and Creating Sponsored Content

As social media marketing continues to grow, partnering with brands and sponsors has become a lucrative opportunity for content creators on X (Twitter). However, successfully negotiating and creating sponsored content requires a strategic approach to ensure authenticity, engagement, and alignment with your audience. This section will explore the key aspects of negotiating sponsorship deals, crafting high-quality sponsored content, and maintaining transparency with your followers.

1. Understanding Sponsored Content on X (Twitter)

Sponsored content refers to posts or campaigns where a brand compensates a content creator to promote a product, service, or event. This compensation can take various forms, including:

- **Direct payments** for tweets, threads, or campaigns.

- **Affiliate partnerships**, where the creator earns commissions based on sales generated through their referral links.

- **Product gifting**, where the brand provides free products in exchange for exposure.

- **Long-term collaborations**, where creators become brand ambassadors and promote the brand over an extended period.

Sponsored content should feel organic, provide value to followers, and align with your usual style and voice. Otherwise, it risks coming across as inauthentic or forced, which can harm credibility and engagement.

2. Finding the Right Sponsorship Opportunities

Before negotiating with brands, it's crucial to ensure that partnerships align with your personal brand, content style, and audience interests. Here are some ways to find the right opportunities:

Identifying Brands That Align with Your Niche

- Look for brands that fit naturally within your content theme (e.g., tech influencers partnering with software companies).

- Consider what products or services your followers would find valuable.

- Avoid brands that may conflict with your values or audience expectations.

Reaching Out to Brands

If brands haven't approached you yet, take the initiative to reach out. Here's how:

- **Craft a Professional Pitch:** Introduce yourself, explain your niche, highlight your engagement metrics, and demonstrate how a collaboration could benefit the brand.

- **Provide Analytics:** Show data such as follower demographics, engagement rates, and past successful collaborations.

- **Suggest a Collaboration Format:** Offer ideas on how you can incorporate their product or service into your content (e.g., reviews, tutorials, creative storytelling).

Joining Influencer Platforms

Many brands use influencer marketing platforms to find content creators. Some platforms that connect brands with influencers on X (Twitter) include:

- Aspire

- Heepsy

- Upfluence

- Influence.co

---

3. Negotiating Sponsorship Deals

Once a brand expresses interest in collaborating, the next step is negotiation. Here are key elements to consider:

Understanding Compensation Models

There are several ways brands may offer compensation, including:

- **Flat Fees:** A one-time payment for a sponsored post.

- **Performance-Based Payments:** Compensation tied to engagement, clicks, or conversions.

- **Affiliate Commissions:** Earnings based on sales generated through your referral links.

- **Equity or Revenue Shares:** A share of company profits instead of direct payment.

Negotiate a payment model that fairly reflects your reach, engagement, and content quality.

Determining Your Rates

Your rate depends on factors such as:

- Audience size and engagement level.

- The effort required to create the content (e.g., single tweet vs. multi-thread).

- Exclusivity agreements (if the brand requires you to avoid promoting competitors).

If unsure about pricing, researching industry benchmarks or consulting other creators can help set competitive rates.

Setting Clear Deliverables

Ensure both parties agree on expectations, including:

- Number of posts or tweets.

- Posting schedule and deadlines.

- Specific messaging, hashtags, or branding elements required.

- Whether revisions or edits are allowed.

Always get agreements in writing to avoid misunderstandings.

4. Creating High-Quality Sponsored Content

Once the deal is finalized, the next step is crafting compelling, engaging sponsored content.

Making Sponsored Content Feel Organic

Avoid making your sponsored posts sound overly promotional or robotic. Instead, integrate the brand naturally into your usual style:

- **Storytelling Approach:** Share a personal experience with the product/service.

- **Educational Approach:** Highlight benefits in a way that informs or entertains your audience.

- **Conversational Tone:** Make the post feel like a recommendation from a friend rather than an ad.

Example of a bad sponsored tweet:
✗ "Buy [Product X] now! It's the best! #Ad"

Example of a good sponsored tweet:
✓ "Been struggling with [problem]? I tried [Product X] and it made a huge difference! Here's what I learned: 📱👇 #Sponsored"

Using Engaging Formats

Different content formats perform better for different audiences. Consider:

- **Single tweets** for quick, impactful messages.

- **Threads** for in-depth storytelling or reviews.

- **Polls and questions** to spark engagement.

- **Videos and GIFs** for visual appeal.

Disclosing Sponsored Content Transparently

To maintain trust and comply with regulations (such as FTC guidelines), always disclose when a post is sponsored. Some common ways to disclose:

- Using **#Ad**, **#Sponsored**, or **#Partner** hashtags.

- Adding a disclaimer such as: "This tweet is sponsored by [Brand], but all opinions are my own."

Hiding sponsorships can damage credibility and even lead to penalties from regulatory bodies.

5. Tracking Performance and Optimizing Future Partnerships

Measuring Engagement Metrics

After publishing sponsored content, track its performance to demonstrate value to brands and improve future collaborations. Key metrics to analyze:

- Likes, retweets, and comments.

- Click-through rates (for affiliate links or product pages).

- Conversion rates (how many users purchased through your promotion).

- Follower growth from the campaign.

Reporting Back to Brands

Most brands appreciate a post-campaign report summarizing performance, such as:

- Screenshots of analytics.

- Audience feedback and reactions.

- Insights on what worked well and suggestions for improvement.

Strengthening Long-Term Brand Relationships

Successful collaborations can lead to repeat business or long-term partnerships. Maintain good communication with brands by:

- Delivering high-quality content on time.

- Providing additional value, such as bonus engagement insights.

- Engaging with the brand's content even outside of paid promotions.

6. Common Pitfalls to Avoid in Sponsored Content

While sponsored partnerships can be highly beneficial, there are some pitfalls to watch out for:

Promoting Products You Don't Believe In

If a product doesn't align with your values or audience interests, avoid promoting it just for money. This can damage credibility and trust.

Ignoring Engagement and Audience Response

Don't just post and forget. Engage with followers' comments, answer questions, and participate in discussions related to the sponsored content.

Overloading Your Content with Sponsorships

Balance organic and sponsored content. If every post is an ad, followers may lose interest. A good ratio is **80% organic content and 20% promotional content**.

Conclusion

Negotiating and creating sponsored content on X (Twitter) is a powerful way to monetize your presence while delivering value to both brands and your audience. The key to success lies in **choosing the right partnerships, negotiating fair deals, crafting authentic content, and engaging with your followers transparently**. By following these strategies, you can build long-term brand relationships while maintaining credibility and growing your online influence.

CHAPTER VI
Best Practices and Common Mistakes

7.1 Do's and Don'ts of X (Twitter)

7.1.1 What Works Best on the Platform

X (formerly Twitter) is a fast-paced social media platform where engagement, visibility, and audience interaction determine success. Understanding what works best on X can help individuals, businesses, and influencers maximize their impact. This section covers essential strategies and best practices that lead to success, including content creation, audience engagement, timing, and platform-specific tactics.

1. Creating High-Quality, Engaging Content

Crafting Attention-Grabbing Tweets

X thrives on brevity. With a 280-character limit, tweets need to be concise yet impactful. Here's what makes a tweet stand out:

- **Clear and concise messaging** – Get straight to the point. Avoid unnecessary filler words.

- **Conversational tone** – Writing as if you're speaking directly to your audience improves engagement.

- **Humor and wit** – Witty and funny tweets tend to get shared widely.

- **Relatable content** – Tweets that reflect everyday experiences or emotions resonate with users.

- **Storytelling** – A compelling story or anecdote draws people in and encourages interaction.

Using Visuals to Increase Engagement

Visual content significantly boosts engagement on X. Tweets with images, videos, or GIFs perform better than text-only posts.

- **Images** – A relevant image can increase tweet engagement by up to 150%. Use high-quality, eye-catching visuals.

- **GIFs** – These add personality and humor to tweets, making them more shareable.

- **Videos** – Short-form videos (30-60 seconds) get high engagement, especially when they provide value, entertainment, or insight.

- **Infographics** – Helpful for presenting data or complex information in an easy-to-digest format.

Writing Effective Threads

Since X has a character limit, threads (a series of connected tweets) allow users to share longer-form content effectively.

- **Start with a strong hook** – The first tweet should grab attention and encourage people to read the rest.

- **Keep it structured** – Numbering tweets (1/10, 2/10) helps readers follow along.

- **Maintain engagement** – Ask questions, use emojis sparingly, and encourage interaction throughout the thread.

- **End with a call to action** – Invite people to like, comment, share, or check out related content.

2. Maximizing Audience Engagement

Encouraging Conversations

Successful X users engage their audience actively rather than just posting content.

- **Ask open-ended questions** – This invites followers to participate in discussions.

- **Respond to comments** – Engaging with replies shows authenticity and builds relationships.

- **Join trending conversations** – Tweeting about current events, viral topics, or industry trends increases visibility.

- **Use interactive elements** – Polls, quizzes, and Q&A sessions encourage audience participation.

Using Hashtags Strategically

Hashtags help categorize tweets and increase their discoverability.

- **Use relevant and trending hashtags** – Research trending hashtags related to your niche.

- **Limit the number of hashtags** – One to three well-chosen hashtags work best; too many can appear spammy.

- **Create branded hashtags** – Companies and influencers can develop unique hashtags to promote campaigns or engagement.

Leveraging Retweets, Mentions, and Quote Tweets

- **Retweet valuable content** – Sharing useful or interesting tweets from others builds connections and credibility.

- **Mention influencers and industry leaders** – Tagging relevant people increases the chances of engagement.

- **Use quote tweets instead of simple retweets** – Adding your own perspective makes retweets more meaningful.

3. Timing and Frequency of Posting

Finding the Best Times to Post

Posting at the right time increases visibility and engagement. While ideal times vary by audience, studies suggest:

- **Morning (8 AM - 10 AM):** Many users check X during their morning routine.

- **Midday (12 PM - 2 PM):** Lunch breaks are a prime time for engagement.

- **Evening (6 PM - 9 PM):** People browse X after work or before bed.

- **Weekdays vs. Weekends:** Engagement is generally higher on weekdays, but weekends can work well for niche audiences.

Maintaining a Consistent Posting Schedule

- **Post multiple times a day** – The fast-moving nature of X means tweets can disappear quickly from timelines.

- **Use scheduling tools** – Tools like Buffer, Hootsuite, or X's built-in scheduling feature help maintain consistency.

- **Balance promotional and engaging content** – Avoid overly promotional posts; focus on value-driven content.

4. Growing Your Audience Organically

Engaging with Like-Minded Communities

Building a following is easier when interacting with users who share similar interests.

- **Join Twitter Communities** – These groups focus on specific topics and provide engagement opportunities.

- **Participate in Twitter Spaces** – Live audio conversations help build authority and connect with an audience.

- **Follow and engage with industry leaders** – Replying to or retweeting their content can boost visibility.

Offering Value to Followers

People follow accounts that provide them with value. This can be in the form of:

- **Educational content** – Sharing industry insights, tips, or news.

- **Entertainment** – Funny memes, witty commentary, or engaging storytelling.

- **Exclusive content** – Providing behind-the-scenes looks, early announcements, or special insights.

Collaborating with Other Users

- **Engage with influencers** – Commenting on their posts can help gain exposure.

- **Cross-promote with others** – Partnering with complementary accounts can help both parties grow.

- **Host giveaways and contests** – These attract new followers and encourage engagement.

5. Utilizing Analytics for Improvement

Understanding Twitter Analytics

X provides insights into tweet performance, audience behavior, and engagement metrics. Key metrics to track include:

- **Impressions** – The number of times a tweet appears in users' feeds.

- **Engagement Rate** – The percentage of interactions relative to impressions.

- **Profile Visits** – How many people visit your profile after seeing a tweet.

- **Follower Growth** – Tracking how your audience expands over time.

Adjusting Strategies Based on Data

- **Identify high-performing content** – Replicate successful tweet styles and topics.

- **Test different posting times** – Experiment to find the most effective schedule.

- **Monitor audience demographics** – Understanding follower interests helps tailor content.

Conclusion

Success on X (Twitter) requires more than just posting content—it's about engagement, strategy, and understanding how the platform works. The best-performing accounts:

1. **Create engaging, high-quality content** using a mix of text, visuals, and storytelling.

2. **Actively engage with their audience** through replies, conversations, and interactive elements.

3. **Use strategic posting practices** such as optimal timing, hashtags, and tweet formatting.

4. **Grow organically** by providing value, joining communities, and collaborating with others.

5. **Analyze performance metrics** and adjust strategies based on data-driven insights.

By applying these best practices consistently, users can maximize their reach, grow their audience, and establish a strong presence on X.

7.1.2 Mistakes That Can Hurt Your Growth

Growing your presence on X (formerly Twitter) requires more than just frequent posting. Many users struggle to expand their audience due to common mistakes that limit engagement, reduce credibility, and even get their accounts flagged or banned. In this section, we will explore the most critical mistakes that can hurt your growth and how to avoid them.

1. Inconsistent Posting Schedule

One of the biggest mistakes users make is being inconsistent with their posting. If you tweet sporadically, your audience will struggle to stay engaged, and the algorithm may not prioritize your content.

How This Affects Your Growth:

- The X algorithm favors accounts that post regularly and engage frequently.

- Long periods of inactivity can cause a drop in visibility.

- Your followers may forget about you if you don't maintain a presence.

How to Fix It:

- Create a content schedule and stick to it.

- Use scheduling tools like Buffer, Hootsuite, or X's built-in scheduling feature.

- Aim for at least 3–5 tweets per day to maintain engagement.

2. Ignoring Engagement and Community Interaction

Many users focus solely on posting content without engaging with others. X is a social platform, and interaction is key to growth.

How This Affects Your Growth:

- People are less likely to engage with your posts if you don't engage with theirs.
- A lack of replies and retweets can make your account seem inactive.
- You miss opportunities to build relationships and increase visibility.

How to Fix It:

- Reply to comments on your posts to keep the conversation going.
- Engage with other users' content by liking, commenting, and retweeting.
- Join discussions and trending topics relevant to your niche.

3. Overusing Hashtags or Using Irrelevant Ones

Hashtags help increase discoverability, but excessive or irrelevant use can backfire.

How This Affects Your Growth:

- Too many hashtags make your posts look spammy.
- The algorithm may deprioritize posts that seem manipulative.
- Using irrelevant hashtags can lead to lower engagement and credibility.

How to Fix It:

- Limit your hashtags to 1–3 per tweet.
- Use relevant hashtags that align with your content.
- Research trending hashtags to maximize reach.

4. Failing to Optimize Your Profile

A poorly set-up profile can discourage people from following you.

How This Affects Your Growth:

- Users may not follow you if they don't understand what you post about.

- Missing a profile picture or bio makes your account seem untrustworthy.

- An unclear or unprofessional username can make it difficult to find you.

How to Fix It:

- Use a clear profile picture and cover image.

- Write a compelling bio that describes who you are and what you post.

- Include a link to your website or other social media accounts.

5. Posting Low-Quality Content

If your tweets lack value, people won't engage with them.

How This Affects Your Growth:

- Poorly written or unoriginal content gets ignored.

- Lack of engagement signals to the algorithm that your content isn't relevant.

- Your followers may unfollow if they don't find your tweets useful.

How to Fix It:

- Share original thoughts, insights, and valuable information.

- Use engaging formats like polls, questions, and visual content.

- Ensure your tweets are grammatically correct and easy to read.

6. Overpromoting Yourself or Your Business

While it's important to promote yourself, doing it excessively can push people away.

How This Affects Your Growth:

- Followers may see your content as spam if every post is a sales pitch.

- A lack of variety in content makes your profile less engaging.

- People follow accounts that provide value, not just advertisements.

How to Fix It:

- Follow the 80/20 rule: 80% valuable content, 20% promotional content.

- Share industry news, tips, and entertaining content alongside promotions.

- Engage with your audience instead of just pushing products or services.

7. Ignoring Trends and Current Events

Trending topics drive engagement, and ignoring them can limit your reach.

How This Affects Your Growth:

- You miss out on high-visibility conversations.

- Your content may feel outdated or disconnected from current discussions.

How to Fix It:

- Keep an eye on the trending section to identify relevant topics.

- Participate in trending conversations with insightful or humorous takes.

- Ensure your input aligns with your brand and audience.

8. Not Using Visual Content

Text-only tweets can get overlooked in a crowded feed.

How This Affects Your Growth:

- Visual content like images, videos, and GIFs increases engagement.

- Users are more likely to share visually appealing posts.

How to Fix It:

- Use high-quality images and videos whenever possible.

- Create eye-catching infographics and short-form videos.

- Use X's native GIF search to add motion to your tweets.

9. Violating X (Twitter) Policies

Breaking platform rules can result in reduced visibility, temporary suspensions, or even permanent bans.

How This Affects Your Growth:

- Algorithm penalties can limit the reach of your tweets.

- Your account could be suspended or banned.

How to Fix It:

- Read and follow X's terms of service.

- Avoid posting hate speech, misinformation, or spam.

- Report inappropriate content instead of engaging with it.

10. Giving Up Too Soon

Many users quit before seeing results, thinking their efforts aren't working.

How This Affects Your Growth:

- Building an audience takes time, and quitting early prevents progress.

- Inconsistent activity leads to decreased visibility.

How to Fix It:

- Set realistic goals for growth and engagement.

- Stay patient and keep experimenting with different content strategies.

- Focus on building genuine connections rather than chasing numbers.

Final Thoughts

Avoiding these mistakes will set you on the path to sustainable growth on X. By staying consistent, engaging with your audience, and adapting to trends, you can maximize your impact and build a strong presence on the platform.

7.2 Security and Privacy Best Practices

7.2.1 Avoiding Scams and Phishing Attacks

X (formerly Twitter) is a powerful platform for communication, networking, and content sharing, but like any social media site, it is also a target for scams, phishing attacks, and cyber threats. Scammers and cybercriminals continuously adapt their tactics to trick users into revealing sensitive information or falling for fraudulent schemes. Understanding these threats and knowing how to protect yourself is essential to maintaining a secure experience on X.

In this section, we will explore the most common scams on X, how phishing attacks work, and the best practices to avoid falling victim to these security threats.

Understanding Phishing Attacks on X

Phishing is a type of cyber-attack where scammers trick users into revealing personal information, such as login credentials, credit card details, or other sensitive data. Attackers often impersonate trusted organizations, such as X itself, well-known brands, or even people you know. Their goal is to steal your information and use it for malicious purposes, such as hacking into accounts or committing financial fraud.

Common Types of Phishing Attacks on X

1. **Fake Login Pages**

   o Scammers send direct messages (DMs) or tweets that contain links to fake login pages that closely resemble X's official login page.

   o When you enter your username and password, the attackers capture your credentials and use them to hijack your account.

2. **Suspicious Direct Messages (DMs)**

   o You may receive a DM claiming that you've won a prize, violated X's policies, or need to verify your account.

- o These messages often include a link leading to a phishing site designed to steal your credentials.

3. **Impersonation Scams**

   - o Cybercriminals create fake profiles that mimic real accounts (such as influencers, businesses, or even X's support team).

   - o They may contact you, requesting sensitive information or offering fake support assistance.

4. **Malicious Links in Tweets**

   - o Fraudsters post tweets with shortened URLs (using services like Bitly) to disguise harmful links.

   - o Clicking these links can redirect you to phishing websites or install malware on your device.

5. **Fake Verification Scams**

   - o You might receive a message offering a verified badge (blue checkmark) in exchange for login details or payment.

   - o X never asks for your password to verify your account, making these scams easy to identify.

How to Identify Phishing Attempts on X

Recognizing phishing attempts is the first step in protecting yourself from falling victim to scams. Here are some red flags to watch out for:

1. Suspicious Links

- If a link looks strange or doesn't match X's official domain (https://twitter.com), avoid clicking it.

- Hover over the link before clicking to see where it actually leads.

2. Urgent or Threatening Messages

- Scammers often create a sense of urgency, claiming your account will be suspended if you don't act immediately.

- X will never send direct messages demanding immediate action through a link.

3. Requests for Personal Information

- Legitimate companies and organizations will never ask for your password via DM or email.

- Be cautious if someone asks for your login credentials, banking details, or security codes.

4. Poor Grammar and Spelling

- Many phishing messages contain spelling mistakes or awkward phrasing, a common sign of fraud.

- Official communications from X are professionally written and free of obvious errors.

5. Unsolicited Prize Announcements

- If you receive a message stating you've won a giveaway you never entered, it's likely a scam.

- Scammers use fake giveaways to lure victims into providing personal information.

How to Protect Yourself from Scams and Phishing on X

Knowing the threats is only part of the solution. To keep your account and personal data safe, follow these best practices:

1. Enable Two-Factor Authentication (2FA)

- Two-Factor Authentication (2FA) adds an extra layer of security by requiring a second verification step when logging in.

- Even if an attacker steals your password, they won't be able to access your account without the second authentication method (e.g., a security code sent to your phone).

- To enable 2FA on X:

  1. Go to **Settings & Privacy**.

  2. Select **Security and Account Access > Security**.

  3. Click on **Two-Factor Authentication** and choose your preferred method (Text message, Authentication app, or Security key).

2. Use Strong and Unique Passwords

- Create a strong password using a mix of uppercase and lowercase letters, numbers, and symbols.

- Avoid using common passwords like "password123" or your name.

- Use a password manager to generate and store complex passwords securely.

3. Be Wary of Unknown Links and Messages

- Never click on suspicious links sent via DMs, emails, or tweets.

- If a link looks suspicious, verify it by checking X's official website or support channels.

4. Verify Accounts Before Interacting

- Before responding to DMs or tweets from businesses or influencers, check if the account is verified.

- Be cautious of newly created accounts impersonating well-known figures.

5. Report Suspicious Activity

- If you receive a phishing attempt, report the account and block the sender.

- To report a scam on X:

  1. Click the **three-dot menu** on the suspicious tweet or profile.

  2. Select **Report Tweet** or **Report Account**.

  3. Choose the appropriate reason (e.g., "It's misleading or deceptive").

6. Regularly Review Connected Apps and Devices

- Cybercriminals can gain access to your account through third-party apps.

- To check and revoke unnecessary permissions:

    1. Go to **Settings & Privacy**.

    2. Select **Security and Account Access** > **Apps and Sessions**.

    3. Remove any apps you don't recognize or no longer use.

7. Stay Updated on X's Security Policies

- X frequently updates its security measures to combat new threats.

- Follow X's official blog or support channels to stay informed about new risks and security best practices.

What to Do If You Fall Victim to a Scam

Even with the best precautions, mistakes can happen. If you believe you've fallen victim to a phishing attack or scam, follow these steps immediately:

1. Change Your Password Immediately

- If you suspect someone has gained access to your account, reset your password immediately.

2. Revoke Unauthorized App Access

- Check your **Connected Apps** and remove any suspicious ones that may have unauthorized access.

3. Enable Two-Factor Authentication (2FA)

- If you haven't already set up 2FA, enable it to add an extra layer of security.

4. Report the Scam to X

- Use X's built-in reporting tools to flag phishing messages or fraudulent accounts.

5. Monitor Your Account Activity

- Regularly check for suspicious activity, such as unauthorized posts, messages, or changes to account settings.

Conclusion

Security on X is an ongoing effort that requires awareness and proactive measures. By understanding how phishing attacks work and following best practices, you can significantly reduce your risk of falling victim to scams. Always stay vigilant, use strong security settings, and report any suspicious activity to help keep the platform safe for everyone.

7.2.2 Protecting Your Account from Hackers

In today's digital age, securing your X (Twitter) account is more important than ever. Hackers use various techniques to steal personal information, spread malicious content, and even impersonate users for fraudulent purposes. A compromised account can lead to serious consequences, including loss of control over your profile, damage to your online reputation, and potential financial loss if connected to monetization features.

This section provides detailed strategies to safeguard your account against cyber threats and ensure a secure online presence.

1. Use a Strong and Unique Password

A weak password is one of the most common ways hackers gain access to accounts. To prevent unauthorized access:

- **Create a Strong Password**: Use a combination of uppercase and lowercase letters, numbers, and special characters. Avoid simple passwords like "password123" or "twitter2024."

- **Make It Unique**: Do not reuse passwords across multiple accounts. If one account is breached, hackers often attempt to use the same credentials on other platforms.

- **Use a Passphrase**: Instead of a single word, consider a longer phrase that is harder to guess, such as "PurpleSunset@2024#isAwesome!"

- **Update Your Password Regularly**: Change your password periodically, especially if X (Twitter) notifies you of any suspicious activity.

💡 **Pro Tip**: Use a **password manager** to securely store and manage your passwords. This helps you avoid the temptation of writing them down or using simple, easy-to-remember passwords.

2. Enable Two-Factor Authentication (2FA)

Two-Factor Authentication (2FA) adds an extra layer of security by requiring a second form of verification beyond your password. Even if a hacker steals your password, they won't be able to access your account without the second authentication step.

How to Set Up 2FA on X (Twitter):

1. **Go to Settings**: Click on your profile picture, go to "Settings and privacy," then navigate to "Security and account access."

2. **Select Two-Factor Authentication**: Choose from three options:

   ○ **Text Message (SMS)**: A one-time code is sent to your phone.

   ○ **Authentication App (Recommended)**: Apps like Google Authenticator or Authy generate secure codes.

   ○ **Security Key**: A physical device used for authentication.

3. **Follow the Setup Instructions**: Complete the process by entering the code provided.

💡 **Best Practice**: Avoid relying on **SMS-based 2FA** alone, as hackers can use **SIM swapping** to intercept text messages. An authentication app or security key is a safer choice.

3. Be Cautious with Third-Party Apps and Permissions

Many users connect third-party applications to their X (Twitter) accounts for added features, such as scheduling tweets or analyzing engagement. However, some apps may pose security risks.

How to Manage Third-Party Access:

- **Review Connected Apps**: Go to "Settings and privacy" → "Security and account access" → "Apps and sessions."

- **Remove Unnecessary Apps**: Revoke access to apps you no longer use or trust.

- **Grant Minimal Permissions**: Only allow apps to access the data they truly need.

💡 **Warning**: Be wary of apps that request excessive permissions, such as the ability to post tweets on your behalf without justification.

---

4. Recognize and Avoid Phishing Attacks

Phishing is a method where hackers trick you into providing your login credentials through fake websites, emails, or direct messages. These attacks often impersonate official X (Twitter) communications.

Signs of a Phishing Attempt:

✓ **Suspicious Links**: Hackers use misleading URLs that look similar to Twitter's official domain (e.g., "tw1tter.com" instead of "twitter.com").
✓ **Urgent Messages**: Beware of messages claiming "Your account will be suspended unless you verify now!"
✓ **Unexpected Login Requests**: X (Twitter) will never ask for your password via email or DM.

How to Protect Yourself:

- **Never Click on Unverified Links**: Always check the sender and URL before clicking.

- **Manually Visit Twitter's Website**: If you receive an email asking you to log in, go to www.twitter.com directly instead of clicking on a link.

- **Enable Login Alerts**: X (Twitter) can notify you when someone logs in from a new device.

💡 **Pro Tip**: If you receive a suspicious email, forward it to phishing@twitter.com for verification.

5. Monitor Your Account Activity

Regularly reviewing your account activity helps you detect and respond to suspicious behavior before it escalates.

Steps to Monitor Your Account:

1. **Check Login History**: Go to "Settings and privacy" → "Security and account access" → "Apps and sessions" to review active sessions.

2. **Log Out from Unrecognized Devices**: If you see an unfamiliar device or location, log out remotely.

3. **Enable Security Alerts**: Turn on email or push notifications for account changes.

💡 **Action Step**: If you notice unauthorized activity, change your password immediately and revoke all active sessions.

6. Protect Personal Information and Avoid Oversharing

The more personal details you share, the easier it is for hackers to impersonate you.

What to Avoid Posting Publicly:

- **Your Email Address**: This makes it easier for hackers to target you with phishing emails.

- **Phone Number**: Unless necessary, avoid making your number public to prevent SIM-swapping attacks.

- **Sensitive Data**: Never share private information, even in DMs, as they can be compromised.

💡 **Best Practice**: Adjust your privacy settings to limit who can see your tweets, send you messages, or tag you in photos.

---

7. Responding to a Hacked Account

If your account is compromised, take immediate action to regain control.

Steps to Recover a Hacked Account:

1. **Reset Your Password**: Use the "Forgot password" feature to create a new, strong password.

2. **Revoke Third-Party Access**: Remove all connected apps that could have contributed to the breach.

3. **Enable 2FA**: If you haven't already, turn on two-factor authentication.

4. **Report to X (Twitter) Support**: Visit the **Help Center** and report a hacked account.

💡 **Emergency Tip**: If you are locked out and cannot recover your password, contact **Twitter Support** immediately to prevent further damage.

Conclusion

Protecting your X (Twitter) account requires a combination of strong security practices, awareness of cyber threats, and regular monitoring. By implementing these best practices, you can significantly reduce the risk of hacking and ensure a safe experience on the platform.

Key Takeaways:

✔ Use a strong, unique password and enable two-factor authentication.
✔ Be cautious with third-party apps and revoke unnecessary permissions.
✔ Stay alert to phishing scams and suspicious login attempts.
✔ Regularly monitor account activity and respond quickly to suspicious changes.
✔ Protect personal information and adjust privacy settings for better security.

By following these steps, you can confidently use X (Twitter) without fear of losing control of your account to hackers. Stay vigilant and enjoy a secure social media experience!

Conclusion

Final Thoughts and Key Takeaways

As we come to the end of this guide, it's essential to reflect on the journey we've taken through the world of X (formerly Twitter). Social media platforms are constantly evolving, and X is no exception. Whether you're using the platform for personal branding, business growth, networking, or just staying updated on global trends, mastering X requires strategy, consistency, and adaptability.

Throughout this book, we've covered everything from setting up an account to engaging with followers, leveraging advanced features, growing an audience, and even monetizing your presence. Now, let's summarize the most crucial takeaways that will help you navigate X successfully.

Understanding X as a Social Media Platform

One of the first things we established is that X is unique among social media platforms. Unlike visual-heavy networks such as Instagram or TikTok, X thrives on real-time conversations, concise content, and viral engagement. Posts (tweets) are limited in character count, forcing users to be clear and impactful with their messaging.

The platform serves a variety of purposes, from news dissemination to business marketing, from casual discussions to professional networking. Your experience on X is largely shaped by how you engage with others, the content you consume and share, and the strategies you implement.

Key Takeaway:

- **X is a fast-paced, text-driven platform where engagement and relevance are key.**

- **Success depends on consistency, high-quality content, and strategic interactions.**

Building a Strong Profile and Presence

Your profile is the first impression people get when they visit your page. A well-optimized profile includes a clear profile picture, an engaging bio, and relevant links. A compelling bio can make a significant difference in attracting followers who resonate with your content.

Once your profile is set up, the next step is building your presence. Content is king on X, and crafting valuable, engaging, and shareable posts is the key to growth. We discussed various types of content that work well, including:

- Text-based insights and opinions

- Thought-provoking questions

- Engaging polls

- Visually appealing images and videos

- Informative threads

Engagement is another critical factor. The more you interact with other users, the more visibility you gain. Liking, retweeting, and replying to other users' posts fosters a sense of community and increases your chances of getting noticed.

Key Takeaway:

- **A well-crafted profile and an engaging content strategy are essential for building your presence.**

- **Consistency and interaction with others boost visibility and credibility.**

Maximizing Engagement and Growth

One of the primary goals for most users on X is to expand their reach and influence. Growing an audience takes time, but there are proven strategies to accelerate the process:

1. **Post Regularly:** Staying active keeps you in your followers' feeds and increases engagement opportunities.

2. **Use Hashtags Strategically:** Hashtags categorize your content, making it discoverable by users searching for related topics.

3. **Engage with Influencers:** Commenting on popular posts and engaging with thought leaders in your niche can expose you to a larger audience.

4. **Participate in Trending Conversations:** Being part of trending discussions can boost visibility and help you gain followers quickly.

5. **Host X (Twitter) Spaces and Polls:** These interactive features allow real-time engagement with your audience.

Additionally, we covered some common mistakes to avoid, such as excessive self-promotion, ignoring audience engagement, and inconsistent posting. Growth is a two-way street—being present and actively contributing to conversations is just as important as posting your own content.

Key Takeaway:

- **Engagement is a two-way process. Actively interact with others while maintaining a consistent posting schedule.**

- **Avoid spammy behavior and focus on adding value to conversations.**

Security and Privacy Best Practices

As with any social media platform, security and privacy should be a priority. We explored the risks associated with scams, phishing attacks, and hacking attempts. Cybercriminals often target social media users, so it's crucial to stay vigilant.

Here are some essential security practices:

- Enable **two-factor authentication (2FA)** to add an extra layer of security to your account.

- Be cautious of **suspicious links** and avoid clicking on unverified messages.

- Regularly **review your connected apps** and remove any that seem unnecessary or suspicious.

- Customize your **privacy settings** to control who can interact with your content.

By implementing these practices, you can protect your account and personal information while safely enjoying the platform.

Key Takeaway:

- **Always prioritize security and privacy settings to protect yourself from scams and hackers.**

- **Enable two-factor authentication and be cautious of suspicious activity.**

Monetization and Business Opportunities

For those looking to turn their X presence into a source of income, there are multiple ways to do so. Whether through influencer marketing, brand partnerships, premium content, or X's monetization programs, the platform offers various opportunities to generate revenue.

Key strategies include:

- **Growing a loyal audience** first before attempting to monetize.

- **Partnering with brands** that align with your niche and audience.

- **Using X Ads** to promote products and services effectively.

- **Leveraging paid subscriptions** through features like Super Follows.

The key to monetization is balancing promotional content with organic engagement. Over-promotion can drive followers away, so it's important to maintain authenticity.

Key Takeaway:

- **Monetization is possible but requires a well-established audience and strategic partnerships.**

- **Focus on providing value before prioritizing revenue generation.**

Final Words: The Future of X (Twitter) and Your Journey

X has evolved significantly over the years, and as a dynamic social media platform, it will continue to introduce new features and policies. Staying updated with platform changes is crucial for maintaining a strong presence.

Your journey on X will be shaped by your goals and the effort you put into engaging with the community. Whether you're here to share insights, build a brand, grow a business, or simply enjoy casual conversations, X offers endless possibilities.

As you move forward, keep these guiding principles in mind:

✓ Stay **authentic**—genuine engagement always wins.

✓ Keep **learning**—social media trends change rapidly.

✓ Be **consistent**—growth takes time but persistence pays off.

✓ **Enjoy the process**—social media should be a tool for connection and creativity.

We hope this guide has provided you with the knowledge and confidence to navigate X effectively. Now it's time to apply what you've learned, experiment with strategies, and find your own path to success on X.

Thank you for reading, and best of luck on your journey!

Acknowledgments

Acknowledgments

First and foremost, I want to express my heartfelt gratitude to you, the reader, for choosing this book. In today's fast-paced digital world, social media is constantly evolving, and learning how to navigate a platform like X (formerly Twitter) is no small task. I truly appreciate your time, trust, and willingness to embark on this journey with me.

Writing this book has been a rewarding experience, but its true purpose is fulfilled only when it helps people like you gain clarity and confidence in using X effectively. Whether you picked up this book as a complete beginner, a business professional, or someone looking to enhance your online presence, I hope it has provided you with valuable insights and practical strategies.

I also want to acknowledge the incredible X (Twitter) community—content creators, industry experts, businesses, and everyday users—who continue to shape the platform into a space for conversation, learning, and connection. Your creativity and engagement serve as inspiration for so many, including myself.

To my friends, colleagues, and supporters who encouraged me throughout the writing process—thank you for your insights, feedback, and belief in this project. Your support has made this book possible.

Lastly, if you found this book helpful, I would love to hear from you! Feel free to connect with me on X and share your thoughts. Your feedback not only helps me grow as a writer but also allows me to continue creating resources that are truly useful.

Thank you again for your time and trust. I wish you all the success in your journey on X and beyond!

Happy tweeting!